TECHNIQUES
FOR DEALING WITH
CHILD ABUSE

TECHNIQUES FOR DEALING WITH CHILD ABUSE

By

ARLENE BAXTER, Ph.D.

Pennsylvania State University
University Park, Pennsylvania
Community College of Allegheny County
Pittsburgh, Pennsylvania

CHARLES C THOMAS • PUBLISHER
Springfield • Illinois • U.S.A.

Published and Distributed Throughout the World by

CHARLES C THOMAS • PUBLISHER

2600 South First Street

Springfield, Illinois 62717

© *1985 by* CHARLES C THOMAS • PUBLISHER

ISBN 0-398-05110-0

Library of Congress Catalog Card Number: 84-26697

Printed in the United States of America

Q-R-3

362.7044
B355t

Library of Congress Cataloging in Publication Data

Baxter, Arlene.
Techniques for dealing with child abuse.

Bibliography: p.
1. Child abuse--United States. 2. Child Abuse--
United States--Investigation. 3. Abused children--
Services for--United States. I. Title. [DNLM:
1. Child Abuse--prevention & control--United States.
WA 320 B355t]
HV741.B35 1985   362.7'044   84-26697
ISBN 0-398-05110-0

To my children, Jeff and Jennifer

INTRODUCTION

A BUSE of children is not a new problem. Historically, society has not been troubled by the maltreatment of children. Where children were not wanted, mortality ran high. In 19th century London, adults sometimes sold children into slavery or used them as sources of cheap labor. Maltreatment of children survived into the late 20th century, virtually unchallenged.

Within the last hundred years, society has begun to shift from the notion of children as their parents' property and the traditional concept of parents' rights to raise their children as they see fit, to the emerging concept of children's rights. The first legal challenge to the absolute rights of parents and children was recorded in New York City in 1870. The history of society's awareness began with the now famous case of Mary Ellen, a child who was unchained from her bed and provided safety away from her patents. This was accomplished because of the persistent efforts of a group of church workers who were able to convince The Society for the Prevention of Cruelty to Animals to act on Mary Ellen's behalf. This case led to the founding of the Society for the Prevention of Cruelty to Children in 1871.

The present interest in the phenomenon of child abuse can be traced to several sources not previously identified with child protective services. In 1961, C. Henry Kempe, a pediatrician, arranged for an interdisciplinary presentation at a meeting of the American Academy of Pediatrics. At this meeting, the term "battered child syndrome" was used to direct attention to the problem.

According to Kempe, the history of the emergence of child abuse as a recognized social issue involves a growing recognition that the maltreatment of children is an unnecessary evil, it requires the technical capability to trace the clues that reveal inflicted injury, and it involves society's readiness to address the problem constructively.

Institutions exist in society for different purposes and on different levels. At the most general level are the universal institutions that express the purposes and values of a society and shape the lives of its members. These universal institutions are significant, for no complex society would function effectively without them.

Basic social institutions are responsible for the general welfare of individuals and communities. They assign and carry out society's tasks, reflect its civic and social values, and provide cultural and recreational opportunities for its members. These include the family, as well as the political, economic, religious, and educational institutions. Of these institutions, the family is the most basic and oldest social unit, whose traces can be found in all societies. Societies depend on the family to socialize their young. As sociologist Talcott Parsons observes

> In socialization the family is above all the agency for establishing cathexis and identification, for integration into the series of social systems in which the child will function as an adult. Above all, perhaps, it is the primary agency for developing his capacity to integrate with others, to trust and be trusted, to exercise influence, and to accept legitimate influence (Parson, 1965).

Every society must make sure that its members conform to most of its expectations. There are many ways in which a society exerts social control on its members (Perry and Perry, 1979). The law is only one, but the preeminent one, of the social controls (Green, 1960). Child abuse has become a phenomenon subject to social control and to a number of laws in the 1980's.

A variety of social service and social control agencies provide the many human services that may be needed at various times by members of the community. Theses include health and day care facilities, child welfare, mental health, and criminal justice agencies (Martin and Klaus, 1978).

Many families may and do avail themselves of these services voluntarily. However, in some cases, society decides to intervene to change individual and family behavior which is defined as deviant and to protect family members who are seen to be a risk, especially children. Society has established specific instruments of social control such as law enforcement, legal institutions, and sanctions which are designed to eliminate or change inappropriate behavior of individuals and families (Martin and Klaus, 1978).

Much has been written in recent years about the battered and neglected child, but the role of law enforcement and the criminal justice system in dealing with the problem has been only marginally explored (Shuchter, 1976). However, it is recognized that an approach regarding child abuse in the 1980's would, of necessity, include the legislative, executive, judical, and the professional practitioner within and outside of the justice system.

As with many of the problems of human need and justice affecting children or adults, it is the availability of institutional services, the legal framework for public intervention, and the nature of professional roles that determine the remedial options provided by society. Once the objectives and strategies have been developed, the key to successful implementation of an approach to the problem of child abuse, intervention processes and procedures, is the training of the professionals involved accompanied by education's efforts aimed at creating an informed citizenry (Shuchter, 1976).

The trend in the law and in the court process seems to be an increasing emphasis on the protection of children's rights. The legal process can go through civil or criminal proceedings. The civil procedure is initiated by a petition which can be filed by anyone, but in most cases, is filed by the agency either receiving or investigating the report of neglect or abuse. State intervention and the judicial decision to intrude into the family relationship for alleged abuse cases are based on a state's abuse and neglect statutes.

Once a case of suspected abuse is reported, community intervention is determined by the agency mandated to receive reports. This varies with different states. An almost universal lack of 24-hour emergency child protective services tends to result in a reliance on the use of law enforcement officers.

Child abuse is often a symptom of a family crisis situation which requires special techniques, skills, and sensitivity for police officers and other professionals to respond appropriately. The police officer's responsibility to the community is to prevent crime, apprehend criminals, ensure public safety, and enforce laws. Police may take part in the initial investigation of alleged cases of child maltreatment since they have the legal authority to gain access to the home and remove the child or abuser from the home. The professional called to assess the scene of suspected child abuse needs the knowledge, the skills, and the training to determine the most appropriate action to fulfill his responsibility to the child, the family, and society.

Children have been physically and sexually abused by adults since the beginning of civilization. What is new regarding this problem is that it has been formally recognized, reporting laws have been mandated, its pathology has been explored, and methods of prevention and treatment have been formulated.

The expansion in the number of agencies and personnel required by law to report child abuse has created many changes. Questions have been raised regarding the competence and training of personnel in keeping with their new responsibilities.

Child abuse is a crime in every state. Some key functionaires in the process of identification and reporting are the professionals who come in contact with children. While some disciplines have specifically trained child abuse personnel, the majority have not. Those teachers, nurses, social workers, and police officers who come in contact with domestic disturbances must be able to assess the problem and identify suspected child abuse. It is imperative that they have the training necessary to evaluate the situation and determine the appropriate action as required by child abuse reporting laws in all fifty states.

The techniques described in this course of study are designed to help professionals understand and manage child abuse incidents in an effective manner.

An increase in the number of agencies and human service personnel required to report suspected child abuse has created many changes. In light of these new developments, the training of professionals has become imperative.

Child abuse and neglect are not solely social, legal, psychological, or medical problems; they should not be managed by one discipline alone. These complex problems involve judges, lawyers, police officers, social workers, physicians, and educators (Gelles, 1975). Five major systems are concerned with child abuse: criminal justice, law enforcement, social service, medicine, and education. The reporting laws in many states require an investigation and report. The professional called upon to assess the scene of suspected child abuse may lack the training and techniques to evaluate the seriousness of the situation and to determine appropriate action for the walfare of the family.

The changing political climate and some recent decisions of the federal courts on the rights of children provide new opportunities as well as a new challenge to professionals and educators for the improved delivery of services to children.

A greater awareness and understanding of sexually and physically abused children and abusive parents by both society and professionals will increase the number of cases reported to Child Protective Services — the ultimate objective being to break the cycle of family violence in society.

CONTENTS

TECHNIQUES FOR DEALING WITH CHILD ABUSE

CHAPTER 1

MODULE I — THE FEELINGS AND ATTITUDES EVOKED BY CHILD ABUSE AND NEGLECT

COURSE OVERVIEW

THIS course of study in the area of child abuse and neglect was designed for use with police personnel and other professionals. The course of study consists of a set of independent modules that may be used alone or in a series, depending on the training objectives and the number of training hours available.

The general purposes of the modules are to train criminal justice personnel to deal more effectively with cases of child abuse and to train personnel in the area of child abuse and neglect to enable them to work in cooperation with other professionals for the welfare of the abused child and the abusive parent. To accomplish these purposes, modules have been designed in the following areas:

1. The attitudes and feelings evoked by child abuse and neglect.
2. An introduction to child development.
3. The identification of child abuse and neglect.
4. Intervention and investigation of child abuse and neglect.
5. The legal parameters of child abuse and neglect.
6. The community resources that deal with child abuse and neglect.
7. The professional's role on multidisciplinary teams dealing with child abuse and neglect.

3

The educational material in the modules is designed to be taught by an educator or instructor experienced in the use of the lecture method for presentation of material; in the use of small and large group discussion techniques to allow for learner participation and feedback; in the case method for the presentation of selected situations and cases for discussion; and in the teaching technique of role-play as a method of revealing the learner's feelings. These teaching skills are a prerequisite to the effective use of the material in the content and method of presentation sections of the modules.

The modules are designed to be taught by an individual or combination of individuals who have the training skills and a knowledge of child abuse in both its factual and attitudinal dimensions.

The modules primary focus is directed toward the police role in all of the content areas, however, the information may be used by all of the professionals who work in the areas of child abuse and sexual abuse. An annotated bibliography is provided for the trainer to enrich his basic knowledge.

Moreover, in meeting the modules' objectives, the trainer may want to use appropriate professionals to deal with the highly specialized content areas of the course of study.

Each module includes a general overview and introductory section, module objectives, content material, suggested method of presentation and, finally, a recommended list of resources for the instructor in the preparation for teaching the module content. The instructor should preview the modules and have the necessary resource materials, i.e. films, copies of laws, case studies, and role profiles as they are needed.

The method of presentation is suggested; however, the instructor should feel confident about using such techniques as discussion groups and role-play before attempting to use them, because success depends on the skillful application of these methods of instruction.

A time frame has been suggested for each module; however, it is flexible and may vary according to the needs of the learners and the instructor. In some instances, assignments are suggested to the instructor at the conclusion of a module in preparation for the following module.

A variety of teaching experiences have been incorporated into the instructional design of the modules. The learning experiences employed take into account the three major criteria described by Tyler. They suggest a group of learning experiences be built on continuity, sequence, and intergration of the presented materials (Tyler, 1971). The teaching techniques used in the design of the modules were selected to increase the learners' substantive knowledge, equip them with new skills, and refine their existing skills and knowledge.

A frequently used teaching method is the lecture, where the speaker is the information source. The effectiveness of lecture is closely related to the organization and presentation of the subject matter. A good lecture should have a central theme relevant to the learner's experience (McKeachie, 1978). In those modules where the lecture method is used, a lecture guideline has been provided. This guide gives some of the major points and subpoints that the trainer may wish to emphasize. However, each trainer will adapt, develop, and modify the lecture content to his needs and the needs of the group. The guidelines should help establish some of the relevent principles to be covered. The lecture method is used in the module for introducing new material, while discussion and group methods are used to achieve other cognitive and affective objectives.

The discussion method used in the modules offers an opportunity for learner participation and immediate feedback. In the modules where the discussion method is recommended, a discussion guideline has been provided along with discussion questions to encourage group participation. The most effective method of achieving affective objectives is the interaction of learners and teachers, in give-and-take discussions. Learners can be motivated and helped to sharpen their judgments and discriminations in order to enable them to deal with new and unpredictable happenings (Kempe, 1971). Cases are provided for use by the trainer in those sessions where they have been suggested. Cases and the accompanying discussion questions may be expanded as the trainer realizes the needs of the groups.

The teaching technique of role playing is used by the researcher as a method of revealing the learner's feeling and attitudes so that they may be examined and discussed by the group (McKeachie, 1978). Role-playing can be an effective teaching device which involves the group directly in a practical learning exercise. Role profiles have been provided.

In the modules where a film is recommended as a teaching aid, the film should be obtained and viewed by the trainer well in advance of its use.

The trainer should review all modules before presentation, so that he may be fully prepared to present the material.

The content and learning experiences of the modules have been designed to help professionals make effective and informed decisions in the disposition of child abuse and neglect cases they may encounter.

MODULE OVERVIEW

This module introduces the topic of child abuse and neglect by presenting society's attitudes and feelings about child abuse throughout history. This provides the background information necessary for an understanding of the problem today, including a basis for the feelings and attitudes evoked by child abuse and neglect. A clarification and understanding of one's feelings and attitudes are explored in relation to one's professional ability to deal with suspected cases of abuse.

In addition to exploring the attitudes of professionals toward child abuse, the attitudes of the abusive family and of society in general will be examined. Just as professionals have preconceived notions and attitudes, prejudices and a mistrust of the intervening agency must also be recognized.

The trainer for Module I, Sessions 2 and 4 should seek out the assistance of a professional in the area of child abuse, psychology, or social work. These professionals in the community who work in the field of child abuse should be called upon to conduct these sessions alone or in combination with the trainer to insure the proper handling of this complex subject area. The content presented here is suggested material for the trainer to use as a frame of reference.

Objectives

1. To increase the trainees' awareness of their personal attitudes and feelings about child abuse and neglect.
2. To examine the trainees' attitudes about child abuse and neglect in relation to their ability to effectively perform their job.

3. To acquire knowledge essential for an understanding of the phenomenon of child abuse and its impact on a family.
4. To identify socio-cultural factors that may contribute to child abuse and neglect.
5. To identify stress patterns and family factors that may contribute to child abuse and neglect.

Schedule

Session 1: Overview and Introduction
Session 2: Attitudes
Session 3: Historical Background of Child Abuse
Session 4: Causation

Session 1: Overview and Introduction

In the opening session, a description and an explanation of the general purposes of the series of modules are given in order to give direction and meaning to the modules so that the students may relate the content to the performance of their duties. An overview of the content areas to be covered in the subsequent modules will be briefly outlined.

Content Material: General Purposes of the Series of Modules

1. To train personnel to deal more effectively with cases of child abuse encountered in the line of duty.
2. To train personnel in the area of child abuse and neglect to enable them to work in cooperation with other professionals for the welfare of the abused child and the abusive parent.

Titles of Modules:

Module I — The Feelings and Attitudes Evoked by Child Abuse and Neglect
Module II — An Introduction to Child Development
Module III — The Identification of Child Abuse and Neglect
Module IV — Intervention and Investigation of Child Abuse and Neglect
Module V — The Legal Parameters of Child Abuse and Neglect

Module VI — The Community Resources that Deal with Child Abuse and Neglect

Module VII — The Professionals Role on Multidisciplinary Teams Dealing with Child Abuse and Neglect

Method of Presentation

The instructor should present the content material to the groups and then allow them time to discuss how this material relates to their work. The needs and suggestions of professionals and training personnel were surveyed and are incorporated into the content areas of the modules. The inherent difficulties of dealing with such an emotionally-charged subject as child abuse and neglect will be acknowledged and discussed. This discussion will lead into the topic of Session 2 which follows.

Session 2: Attitudes

This session involves a general discussion of the feelings and attitudes which are an integral part of child abuse and neglect.

All professionals, especially police, must be aware of their attitudes about both the abusers and the abused in order to recognize the difficulty of the subject for everyone. Moreover, they must be aware of society's attitude toward the professional in this context. This recognition will help to minimize the adverse effects of negative attitudes on the investigation process. An individual's attitudes reflect the societal milieu. A brief introduction to this concept will lead into the correlation between society's historical view of children and the incidence of child abuse.

Content Material: Discussion Questions

1. What do you think constitutes neglect and abuse? Briefly refer to the legal definition.
2. What experiences have you had involving cases of child abuse and neglect?
3. What kinds of attitudes about child abuse and neglect have you encountered in dealing with these cases?
4. What are some of your feelings concerning abused children and abusive caretakers?

5. Do your attitudes toward child abuse and neglect cases differ from your attitudes toward other kinds of cases? If so, how? If not, why?
6. Do you think a professional's attitudes affect his/her ability to investigate child abuse and neglect cases? If so, how? If not, why?
7. How can one lessen the effect of a judgmental attitude on his/her professional ability to conduct investigations of child abuse and neglect cases?

Method of Presentation

A group discussion about the general personal attitudes concerning abused children and abusive parents will make the group more aware of these feelings and how they may affect the performance of their jobs. Discussion should be encouraged regarding one's feelings about the abusive parent and how they may affect the course of case disposition. An examination is made of how to direct anger toward ways of providing more lasting protection for a child. Actual cases and examples described by the student enhance the group's awareness of how one's attitudes and feelings may cloud the issues in question.

Session 3: Historical Background of Child Abuse

Background information is presented that relates the attitudes and values of society regarding children with the actual treatment of children. The lecture will point out that the maltreatment of children has existed for centuries and was condoned as a way of controlling, educating, discipling, and using children to achieve some societal goal. Historically, society has not been troubled by the maltreatment of children, and it has continued and thrived. The following lecture material should be preceded by an introduction which may be interrupted by comments, questions, and discussions. A summary should follow the lecture.

Content Material: Lecture Guidelines

I. Historical attitudes towards children.
   A. In the past, society has not been troubled by the maltreatment of children.

1. In 19th century London, adults sold children into slavery.
2. In 19th century England, children were used as a cheap source of labor.
3. Until late into the 20th Century, maltreatment of children was prevalent because (a) children were considered to be the property of their parents, (b) physical punishment was seen as necessary to maintain discipline and to rid children of evil spirits.
4. Children have been considered an expendable commodity throught history.
5. Children have been exploited, overworked, slain by their parents without social criticism.

II. A change in society's views regarding children resulted from affluence, from the mortality rate and from the child welfare movement.
   A. Child abuse awareness began only about 100 years ago.
      1. In a famous case, Mary Ellen was unchained from her bed and given refuge away from her parents.
      2. Help was provided by extending the protection of the Society for the Prevention of Cruelty to Animals to include children.
      3. This led to the establishment of the Society for the Prevention of Cruelty to Children in New York in 1875.
      4. 1860 — Ambroise Tardieu, Professor of Legal Medicine in Paris identified child abuse as a prevailing cause of death.
      5. 1946 — John Caffey investigated and identified abnormal x-ray changes in children. Caffey and Silverman investigated and attributed their findings to abuse.
      6. 1961 — C. Henry Kempe directed attention to the problem at an interdisciplinary presentation at the annual meeting of the American Academy of Pediatrics. At this time, the term "Battered Child Syndrome" was introduced.

III. Research on child abuse
    A. Research in child abuse was done by Elmer and Reinhart at Pittsburgh's Childrens Hospital.
        1. Kempe, Elmer, Caffey, and Silverman were some of the people who did report the facts about child abuse in society.

IV. Future goals
    A. In order for child abuse and neglect to emerge as a recognized social issue we must have:
        1. A recognition that the maltreatment of children as wrong.
        2. The technical capability to trace the clues that ultimately reveal a story of inflicted injury.
        3. The communities readiness to address the problem in a constructive manner.
        4. Recognition of the importance of human growth and development.
        5. Children's Rights and Child Advocacy Law.

Method of Presentation

During this session, the lecture method is used to present the historical background of child abuse and neglect. A discussion and summary should follow the lecture. A closing statement should point out that the attitudes of society and the communities readiness to act on the issue of child abuse and neglect is closely tied to the need for education and an understanding of abused children and their abusive parents. Mention should be made of the fact that child abuse has been ignored or denied by many professionals for a variety of reasons. Professionals not wanting to acknowledge the presence of abuse have tended to overlook its signs. Family physicians are reluctant to place themselves in a role where they must perform a disciplinary function.

There is suspicion that the high reported incidence of abuse among law socioeconomic social class may reflect racial bias. Material relating to this will be explored in subsequent modules.

Emphasize the fact that the failure to recognize and report abuse cases still exists today. Relate this to the police experiences with doctors and neighbors who refuse to get involved in cases of child abuse and neglect, despite the immunity clause in the reporting law. Moreover, individuals' attitudes reflect society's attitude. This concept will lead to a discussion of the correlation between society's view of children and maltreatment of children and to the discussion in Session Four of the suggested causes of child abuse and neglect.

Session 4: Causation

This session deals with some of the causes of child abuse and neglect. Session 1 presented an overview of the series of modules, their purposes and the material to be covered. Session 2 explored the emotional impact of child abuse and neglect with concentration on the learner's feelings and how they may interfere with job performance. Session 3 provided a look at these attitudes and feelings in light of the role of children throughout history. Session 4 deals with the attitudes and values in society which influence individual and family relationships. Child abuse and neglect have been considered an extreme response to these stresses. A professional in the area of child abuse should be called in to conduct or assist the trainer in conducting this session.

Content Material: Lecture Guidelines

I. Extent of Abuse.
   A. The extent of child abuse and neglect is not known.
      1. It occurs in the privacy of the home and is often unreported.
      2. A number of estimates concerning the incidence of abuse range from 500,000 to 4.5 million. The National Center on Child Abuse and Neglect estimates 1 million children are maltreated by their parents each year. From 60,000 to 100,000 are sexually abused, and from 100,000 to 200,000 are physically abused. The remainder are neglected, and 2,000 children die in circumstances that suggests abuse or neglect.
II. Causes of Abuse.
   A. No one factor leads to child abuse and neglect; a variety of

causes include severe emotional pressures, a family history of violence, and the burdens resulting from poverty.

1. Multiple forces on the family reinforce each other and cause abuse and neglect.
2. Individual causal factors may include physical health, mental health, intelligence, personality, previous life experiences, and socialization.
3. Cultural forces are incorporated in an individual's attitudes and values, and they affect family relationships.
4. Societal forces include attitudes toward children, changing family roles, violence and corporal punishment, economic and social competition, and religion.
5. Situations which effect parents' relationships with their children, such as marital relationship, jobs, money, and amount of social contact reinforce other family problems.

III. Abusive Families

A. Abusive parents may be suffering individuals; many were abused themselves as children.

1. Abuse and neglect take place among the rich as well as the poor.
2. Abuse is more highly visible among the lower classes.
3. The rich seem to be more susceptible to internal stress since their physical needs are satisfied.
4. The poor are more exposed to life's external stresses.

IV. Help for Abusive Families

A. Kempe's research has concluded that only in about 10 percent of the reported cases of abuse and/or neglect is there evidence of an abnormal, psychotic, or criminal parent who cannot be helped.

1. The majority of abusive parents need to be helped to balance the needs of his child with his own needs in times of stress.
2. In a time of crisis when life stresses become too great, a parent may revert to the violence that he knew from his parents as a child. Therefore, a cycle of violence may continue unless intervention occurs.

V. Attitudes toward Abuse

    A. A greater awareness and understanding of abused children by both society and professionals are important goals.

        1. One's attitudes about abusive parents and their actions must be understood and admitted.

        2. Some long-standing personal attitudes must be dealt with by professionals in order for them to feel free to report suspected cases of abuse and neglect.

Discussion Questions:

1. Do you see child abuse and/or neglect as crossing socioeconomic lines?
2. Do you feel that a connection exists between violence in the streets and violence in the home?
3. How do you feel about the statement that abusive parents feel a burden of guilt?
4. Do you feel that a discrepancy exists between the reported incidence of abuse and neglect and the actual incidence of abuse and neglect?

Method of Presentation

A recap of the previous sessions' main topics will serve as a review and will lead into the new material. The lecture method is used in Session 4 to inform the learners of the many factors involved in child abuse and neglect. A group discussion should follow the lecture to answer any questions its content may provoke and to relate the lecture to the learners' experiences.

Before the presentation of Module II — Introduction to Child Development, the instructor should give the learners an assignment, the observation of children. The learners may be divided into groups responsible for observing children at a certain age: infants, toddlers, primary school age, and elementary school age children.

Resources: Required for the Instructor as Background for Teaching Module I

1. Fontana, V.S., *Somewhere a Child is Crying*: Maltreatment, Causes

and Prevention. New York: MacMillan Publishing Company, 1973.

This book discusses the "battered child syndrome" and its causes. Articles about families in stress, failure of the courts to act quickly and recognizing neglected children are included. Case studies are presented to illustrate certain points. Suggestions for establishing preventive programs are given.

2. Kempe, C.H. and Helfer, R.E. (Eds.), *Helping the Battered Child and His Family*. Philadelphia: J.B. Lippincott Company, 1972.

This book defines and describes the various categories of abuse. It deals with the problem of abuse and suggests an approach to the attitudes, the prevention of abuse and the treatment of abusive families.

3. Kempe, R.S., and Kempe, C.H., *Child Abuse*. Cambridge: Harvard University Press, 1978.

This book is helpful in exploring sexual abuse in addition to physical abuse. The authors explain that although attaching blame to the parents may be an initial reaction, it is more useful to view their behavior as an extreme response to stress.

4. Gil, D.G., *Child Abuse and Violence*. New York: A.M.S. Press Incorporated, 1979.

This series of articles gives insight into individual, institutional and societal violence and into the needs, rights, and development of children. Many of the articles link child abuse to the larger issues of violence in society using examples of family violence and corporal punishment in child rearing.

5. Helfer, R.E., and Kempe, C.H., (Eds.), *The Battered Child*. Chicago: The University of Chicago Press, 1980.

The contributors to *The Battered Child* concern themselves with such issues as who are abused children, what are their backgrounds, and can their abuse be prevented? This book covers the history, incidence, reporting, intervention, and treatment of cases of abuse. The role and responsibility of law enforcement are included.

6. Johnson, D., *Interpersonal Effectiveness and Self Actualization in Reaching Out*. Englewood Cliffs: Prentice Hall Incorporated, 1972.

In this book the author explores interpersonal relationships and attitudes. The material would be helpful in understanding and handling the affective content areas to be presented in Module 1.

7. Simon, S., And Howe, L.W., and Kirshen Gaum, *Values Clarification — A Handbook of Practical Strategies for Teachers and Students*. New York: Hart Publishing Company, 1978.

This handbook presents a series of exercises for bringing about the recognition of one's attitudes and values. This would be helpful in exploring the feeling and attitudes evoked by child abuse and neglect.

CHAPTER 2

MODULE II — AN INTRODUCTION TO CHILD DEVELOPMENT

MODULE OVERVIEW

THIS module provides a basic time line of the "average" child's developmental stages. Life stages and their age-appropriate behaviors are described and discussed in order to build a frame of reference for comparing and identifying abused and neglected children. Because of the specific nature of the content in this area, a guest speaker from the field of child development, psychology, or pediatric medicine would be advantageous. A speaker from one of these areas should be invited to assist the trainer for several reasons: (1) He would be well qualified to trace the physical development of a child. (2) He would be able to answer the technical questions of the group. (3) He would bring an element of practical experience to the discussion. (4) His interacting with the learners would provide some much needed support between disciplines. (5) He would contribute a knowledge of his discipline's role in helping abused and/or neglected children. (6) Cooperation between professionals might help untangle the complexities of child abuse and neglect. The trainers' role throughout the module will be to assist the child development professional in intergrating the human growth and development material with the needs of the learners.

A professional called to the scene of a domestic disturbance may find evidence of child abuse or neglect. His suspicions of abuse will be based on his observations. These observations in large part will be influenced by a knowledge of what is age-appropriate behavior for the child in question.

Objectives

1. To acquire a basic knowledge of the age-appropriate behaviors of childhood to help in identifying abused and neglected children.
2. To identify possible areas of permanent and serious damage caused by child abuse and neglect in relation to the physical, emotional and mental development of the child.
3. To develop an awareness of changing family roles as they relate to child development.
4. To develop an awareness of changing attitudes toward children, as they pertain to child development.
5. To recognize a family's stress factors as related to child abuse and neglect causation.

Schedule:

Session 1: Child Development and the Family
Session 2: Effects of Abuse on Development
Session 3: Parental Role

Session 1: Child Development and the Family

This session introduces the topic of child development to the group. In this opening session of Module II, an introduction to the topic of Child Development is given. An overview of the module contents and objectives at this time will familiarize the learners with the material to be covered. The overview will also relate the content material to the job of the learner making the discussion a more meaningful learning experience.

Without a basic knowledge of normal child development, one cannot identify the neglected or abused child's physical and emotional problems. In addition to physical development, emotional development and needs should be correlated to give a more complete picture of growth. The following material may be used as a framework for the trainer, or the lecturer in child development, to develop and augment.

Content Material: Discussion of Module Objectives

I. Module Objectives
  A. To acquire a basic knowledge and understanding of child development.
    1. Discuss the need for this knowledge as it relates to the work of the police officer involved in a domestic call.
  B. To acquire a basic knowledge of the age-appropriate behaviors of childhood.
  C. To identify possible areas of permanent and serious damage caused by child abuse and neglect in relation to the physical, emotional, and mental development of the child.
    1. This area will be discussed at length in the second session.
    2. This will lend continuity to the sequence of sessions and point out how they build on previous learnings.
  D. To develop an awareness of changing family roles as they affect a child's development.
  E. To develop an awareness of changing attitudes toward children.
  F. To recognize a family's stress factors as related to child development and child abuse.

Introductory Discussion:

Case #1:

You are responding to a call concerning an alledged neglected child. Upon entering an unlocked house, you find the only occupant is a small child in a filthy crib. Soon, the child's mother appears in the doorway. She explains that she has just been gone for a short while and that the 1-½-year-old rarely moves, so she felt it was safe to leave her in the crib.

In what way would a knowledge of the normal development of a 1-½-year-old help the officer make an appropriate decision?

Case #2:

You are responding to a domestic call involving an alleged fight between a man and his wife. When you arrive on the scene, the fight has ended, but you observe a child cowering in a corner of the room obviously afraid of the adults in the room.

In what way would a knowledge of child development aid the officer in determining whether the child was at risk?

Case #3:

You are responding to a domestic call involving an alleged case of neglect. A neighbor reported that Mr. and Mrs. Johnson have a young son who has not been heard from or seen by anyone in several weeks. The child was reported to be 11 months old and never utters any sounds. The neighbor feared that something was wrong because the Johnson's would not answer any questions about the "disappearance" of their son. When you arrive on the scene, Mr. Johnson welcomes you and shows you the crib where the baby is sleeping. Mrs. Johnson is very quietly sitting in a chair staring at the wall. You observe the very still child who is extremely tiny and frail. The apartment is neat, too neat and sparsely furnished for the middle-class neighborhood. The child is not battered, but the environment seems strained to the keen observer.

In what way would a knowledge of child development and the impact of environment on development aid the officer in determining if this might be a case of failure to thrive?

Case #4:

You are responding to a domestic call involving an alleged fight between a woman and her boyfriend. When you arrive on the scene, the man is firing a gun and threatening the woman. When the smoke has cleared, the man is removed from the house, and the woman is fearful but calm. A small child wanders out from a back bedroom visibly shaken by what has taken place. The child has not been involved in the scuffle, but according to the neighbors, she is constantly exposed to this kind of an environment.

In what way would knowledge of the impact of environment on emotional development aid the officer in determining the appropriate disposition in this case?

The following material concentrates on the growth and development of the young child. Because of the inability of the infant and young child to communicate his needs or problems accurately, he may frequently be the target of abuse and in need of protection. An officer called to the scene of a domestic call should be aware of normal patterns of growth and development in order to be more alert to signs of arrested development that may be the result of abuse and/or neglect.

Outline for the Blackboard:

Child Development Year:
- 0-1   eye control, head, arm and hand control, and late in the first year, leg and feet control.
- 1-2   walks, runs, says words, and phrases, may begin bowel and bladder control. A sense of identity and possession.
- 2-3   sentences, thoughts, understands his environment and can comply with some cultural demands.
- 3-4   asks questions, can generalize and conceptualize — self-dependent at home.
- 5   by age 5, child is well matured in motor control, can hop, skip, speak clearly, enjoys play, feels socialized pride, a citizen of his small world.

Child Development Lecture:

The following material is not intended to make experts of the learners but to familiarize them with the needs of growing children. It will also examine the impact of a positive and negative environment on the developing child. This will serve as a frame of reference in helping the learner to identify cases of neglect that may not be as apparent as cases of physical abuse.

The focus in this module is on those developmental stages which preceed adolescence. Content related to adolescence and post adolescence as it relates to both physical and sexual abuse will be dealt with in Modules III and VII.

   I. Developmental Periods
     A. The major developmental periods are:
       1. Prenatal period: may be affected by mother's health habits, drugs, smoking, etc.
       2. Infancy: (refer to resource chart.)
       3. Babyhood: A stage which goes from dependency (two

weeks to two years) to an attitude of independence.

4. Early Childhood: the child is dependent on family and home environment.

5. Adolescence: preparation for adulthood.

II. Individual differences in children.

  A. Development is influenced by environment as well as by hereditary potential.

    1. Unfavorable environmental conditions can alter this pattern either temporarily or permanently.

    2. Deviations from the normal patterns of physical development may be accompanied by deviations in psychological development.

    3. Poor health, inadequate nutrition, emotional deprivation, lack of motivation to learn, etc. may affect the normal growth rate.

    4. Emotional deprivation may result in personality distortions.

III. Understanding a baby's physical needs.

IV. Understanding a baby's equally important psychological needs.

V. Meeting Needs

  A. The satisfaction of the child's needs gives the baby a sense of the world as a good, stable and ultimately manageable place.

    1. Basic trust is developed.

VI. Unmet Needs

  A. When the child's needs are not met.

    1. The world becomes a threat and frustration results.

    2. The child develops a basic mistrust of the world around him.

The film, *Those First Years*, is recommended for use at this time. It shows behaviors which exemplify important concepts in the early years of life: physical behaviors, emotional behaviors, and the beginning of indepent behaviors. This film is 17 minutes long and is available in the Pittsburg area through the Western Psychiatric Institute Audiovisual Library. It is produced by the National Medical Audiovisual Center in cooperation with Nell Hodgson Woodruff

School of Nursing. The film should be obtained and previewed by the trainer well in advance of its use as a teaching aid in Module II, Session 1.

Method of Presentation

If the recommended assignment was given at the close of Module I, it should be followed up at the beginning of Module II. Each group will be asked to report on their observations as an introduction to the topic of child development.

A variety of introductory discussion cases are used to show how a knowledge of child development can aid a police officer in identifying child abuse and neglect. The questions which accompany each case will begin the discussion about the case. The learners' own experiences with domestic calls will follow. Child abuse and neglect are often a product of domestic violence.

Before the session begins, a brief time line of the growth and development of an infant should be written on the blackboard. This will serve as a focal point for the discussion and reinforce the concepts to be presented. The blackboard outline and a lecture on the subject of child development will serve as an introduction to the film, *Those First Years*. A discussion of the main points of the film and an opportunity to answer questions will follow the showing. The trainer should emphasize that individual differences exist in the growth and developmental stages of childhood and that the time line presented is flexible. Only a brief introduction to the film will be needed since the time line and lecture will prepare the learners for the material presented in the film. However, a summary of the main points of the film should follow its viewing.

The trainer should familiarize himself with "normal" child developmental patterns in contrast to the arrested developmental patterns of abused and neglected children presented in later session.

Session 2: Effects of Abuse on Development

In this session, a contrast is made between the abused child and the child who has not been abused. The learnings of the previous session on normal development will be reviewed in the light of the arrested development found by researchers in abused and neglected children. The abuse of one's child is usually not a premeditated decision but an irrational act followed by the abusive parent's grief and guilt. For this reason, the trainer must refer to the session on attitudes to review the importance of understanding and clarifying one's own attitudes about abusive parents. Negative attitudes and ignorance of the problems involved in child abuse and neglect make a considerable differenc in how one approaches it.

Content Material: Lecture Guidelines

I. Effects of child abuse that may be observed by a professional.
   A. Child abuse and neglect can result in permanent and serious damage to the child.
      1. Physical damage may be the result of beating or other forms of physical abuse.
      2. Emotional damage can be the devastating result of living in an atmosphere created by abuse.
      3. The normal mental development of the child can be arrested or retarded because of abuse.

II. Physical Abuse.
   A. The physical effects of child abuse.
      1. Physical abuse may result in damage to the brain, vital organs, eyes, ears, arms or legs.
      2. Injuries may result in mental retardation, blindness, deafness, or loss of a limb.
      3. Both child abuse and neglect may result in the death of a child.

III. Emotional and Cognitive Effects.
   A. Child abuse and neglect are often as damaging emotionally as they are physically.
      1. Abused or neglected children may be impaired in the areas of self-concept, ego competency, reality testing, and overall thought process.
      2. They may have a higher level of aggression and anxiety and a lower level of impulse control.
      3. These characteristics can cause abused or neglected children to display high levels of antisocial or criminal behavior as they get older.

　　4. Abuse and neglect may also result in restricted cognitive development.
　　5. Language, perceptual and motor skills are often undeveloped, further limiting the child's chances to succeed.

IV. The Abused Child.
　A. The abused child may love his parents and turn to them for love despite what an observer may label an intolerable situation.
　　1. How much positive attention the child receives and how much abuse may depend on his ability to adapt to his parent's expectations.
　　2. Abused children may be constantly alert and vigilant to avoid trouble and above all to please.
　　3. Abused children have been known to be very compliant and resigned.
　　4. They always seem aware of the possibility of physical punishment.
　　5. These children tend to react more normally in a nonthreatening environment. However, they are reluctant to show how lonely and frightened they are.
　　6. An abused or neglected child takes a long time to learn to trust people.

Method of Presentation

During this session, the lecture method is used to present the effects of abuse on a child's development. With this as a background, a discussion of the effects of neglect and/or abuse should be approached. At this point, a brief contrast of normal and arrested development will reinforce the learning. Some of the characteristics of abused and neglected children referred to in the lecture should be repeated, and the learners should be asked to relate their experiences with cases of abuse they may have encountered. The trainer should relate these personal experiences of the class to important points in the lecture.

A closing statement should refer to the attitudes and feelings evoked by child abuse and neglect. The trainer should emphasize the importance of being familiar with normal development in order to identify more accurately the arrested development resulting from abuse cases. Abuse does not take place in a vacuum, and changing family roles and parental stress will be discussed in Session 3.

Session 3: Parental Role

The subject of the parental role in child development may be introduced in the context of family dynamics. The effects of a loving, trusting environment for an infant are contrasted with the effects of one where fear of physical punishment is constant. The long range psychological and emotional effects on an abused and/or neglected child's development are reviewed. Family patterns that produce stressful situations leading to abuse are explored and dealt with. The material in this session will help to alert professionals to the possibility of child abuse and neglect in a variety of situations. Some indicators of "high-risk parents" are examined and related to child development. These high-risk indicators are examined in more detail in Module III. This brief introduction will provide continuity of content.

Content Material: Lecture Guidelines

I. Dynamics of Abusive Families.
   A. No single factor can account for an abusive parent's behavior.
      1. Abuse occurs as a result of several interlocking factors that precipitate a crisis or stress situation.
      2. In time of crisis, the abuse of a child occurs, in many cases, because he is a helpless, natural target.
      3. A parent may see their child as not loveable or as a disappointment.
      4. No effective support system in time of crisis can be a contributing factor.
      5. The abused child may be incorrectly perceived by the parents.
      6. In an abusive family, the parents needs come before those of the child.
      7. Many abusive parents may have unrealistic expecta-

tions of their children and of the developmental process.

II. Problems of Abused and Neglected Infants in the Context of Family Dynamics.
  A. Neglect and prolonged malnutrition can do permanent damage to an infant's development.
    1. In a home where neglect persists, an infant learns very early in life that his needs will not be met.
    2. In contrast, a sense of trust in the environment is learned by a child whose needs are met by family and/or care providers.
    3. The conditions for developing basic trust or mistrust in a child varies within well meaning families.
    4. Compare this with conditions that exist in homes of abused children.

Method of Presentation

The lecture method is used to present material on the parental role in child development as viewed in the larger context of family dynamics.

In this session, a case study is used to encourage class discussion and reinforce the material presented in the lecture. An introduction to this case study should be preceded by a discussion of the term "high-risk parent". High-risk parents are those who have a high potential for either abusing or neglecting their children. The degree of risk for a child depends upon the parents potential to abuse, on the child himself, and on the occurrence of a crisis situation or precipitating event. All of these factors will be further explored in Module III. Copies of the case study should be distributed to the group. After the group has read the case and considered its contents, the questions may be used to stimulate class discussion of the important points.

Resource Material:

Case #1:

Mary was an attractive 17-year-old high school student dating John, also a 17-year-old high school student. They both came from a low socioeconomic background. Mary came from a single parent home; her Dad had died in a construction accident when she and her younger brother were very young. Her mother had worked outside the home for as long as Mary could remember. When her mother was home, the arguments seemed never ending. Mary began dating at about 14 and now at 17, was seeing John often. Shortly after Mary became pregnant, she and John married. Mary was hardly ready for marriage, but the prospect of motherhood seemed like fun. After marriage, John preferred playing ball or drinking at the local bar to being home at night with Mary. So, trouble began even before their child was born.

After Gary, their son, arrived, things seemed better. John stayed home to show off his new son, but he refused to participate in any way in his care. Mary complained constantly about the lack of money, about the crying baby, about John's lack of interest in her, and about the lack of fun in her life. John could get out all day while she was stuck in with Gary. John's parents visited occasionally, but they were still unhappy about the marriage. Mary's Mom rarely came to see her. Having no idea of how Gary should behave, Mary was often irritated by his behavior. She felt he cried too often, was wet too often, and demanded too much of her time. When Gary cried, Mary screamed. When John began staying out longer and more frequently, her anger at being tied down became more intense. Soon yelling at Gary didn't quiet him, so she would lift him from the crib and shake him. When that failed, she used increasingly harsher forms of dicipline. Although abused on a regular basis, Gary had never been taken for treatment. During his occasional visits to the doctor for shots, Mary explained Gary's bruises with stories of his being accident-prone.

When Gary was 18 months old, he had a cold and refused to eat or sleep. The crying became intolerable for Mary and, as usual, John was absent. When slapping and punching failed, Mary severely beat Gary, however, she couldn't ignore the sight of the limp child, and she took him to the hospital emergency room. This time, the case of abuse could not be hidden, and a report was filed.

Discussion Questions:

1. What were some of the interacting factors involved in this case of abuse?

2. What are some of the social, cultural, or religious factors that may have been involved in this case?
3. How does the knowledge of child development enter into case?
4. What support systems were or were not available to Mary?
5. What do you think were some of John's feelings about his marriage?
6. What do you feel about Mary's expectations of the marriage?
7. Can you sympathize with John or Mary regarding their feelings about their marriage?

Resources: Required for the Instructor as Background for Teaching Module II

1. Elmer, E., *Fragile Families Troubled Children*. Pittsburgh: University of Pittsburgh Press, 1977.

This descriptive study of abused and accident children and their families was designed to identify possible physical, developmental, and behavioral differences between abused and non-abused infants. After an initial infant study, a follow-up was done one year later and a second follow-up eight years later.

2. Gesell, A., and Amatrude, C.S., *Normal and Abnormal Child Development*, 2nd edition. New York: Harper & Row Publishers, 1967.

This book explores the abnormal as well as the normal process of a child's development. The influences of both biology and culture on the developmental growth pattern are discussed, providing the trainer with a contrast of normal and abnormal developmental patterns.

3. Hurlock, E.B., *Child Development*. 4th edition. New York: McGraw Hill Company, 1956.

This basic child development text will serve as background for the trainer and increase understanding of physical growth patterns of children from birth to adolescence.

4. James, H., *The Little Victims*. New York: David McKay Company, Incorporated, 1975.

This book reports on a study of sixty abused, thirty neglected, and thirty "normal" children in New York City. The study revealed greater depression and aggressive tendencies in the abused group. James discusses a correlation between these aggressive tendencies and later delinquent behavior.

5. Stone, J.L., and Church, J., *Childhood and Adolescence. The Psychology of the Growing Person*. New York: Random House, 1973.

Concentrating on the emotional and psychological development of childhood and adolescence, this text will be helpful in contrasting "normal" development with the arrested development of abused and neglected children. A film, "Those First Years," produced by National Medical Audiovisual Center in cooperation with Nell Hodgson Woodruff School of Nursing is available in Pittsburgh through Western Psychiatric Institute Audiovisual Library.

CHAPTER 3

MODULE III — THE IDENTIFICATION OF CHILD ABUSE AND NEGLECT

MODULE OVERVIEW

THIS module presents a description of physical abuse, neglect, and sexual abuse. Emphasis will be placed on the physical and behavioral indicators of child abuse and neglect which can be used in the identification process. This module is concerned with an informed professional's recognition of the physical and behavioral signs of abuse and neglect.

The trainer for Module III should seek out the assistance of professional in the area of child abuse, medicine, or social work. One or a combination of these professionals should conduct or help to conduct the sessions in Module III. An experienced professional, helping the trainer, will insure the proper presentation of this complex subject matter. The material presented here is suggested for the trainer to use as a frame of reference.

Objectives

1. To identify the physical conditions of suspected child abuse and neglect.
2. To identify the behavioral indicators of child abuse and neglect.
3. To identify the physical indicators of sexual abuse.
4. To identify the social and family factors that may contribute to abuse and neglect.

Schedule:

Session 1: Recognizing Child Abuse and Neglect
Session 2: Physical Indications of Child Abuse and Neglect
Session 3: Behavioral Indicators of Abuse and Neglect
Session 4: Sexual Abuse and its Indicators

Session 1: Recognizing Child Abuse and Neglect

The first session of Module III begins with an overview of the module including the content areas to be covered as well as the course objectives.

Child abuse and neglect can be divided into four major areas: Physical abuse, neglect, sexual abuse, and emotional maltreatment. Each of these areas has some recognizable indicators that may be encountered by the professional. The learner should be aware of the physical and behavioral indicators of the various types of child abuse and neglect he may encounter. This module focuses on the indicators of child abuse and neglect which can be used in the identification process when physical or sexual abuse is suspected.

In many instance, a police officer is the first to arrive on the scene of a complaint of abuse. A skilled observation of the home at this time can be more valuable than a visit by appointment later. Such an observation may provide a candid evaluation of the home environment.

Content Material: Module Objectives

1. To identify the physical conditions of suspected child abuse and neglect.
2. To identify the behavioral indicators of child abuse and neglect.
3. To identify the physical indicators of sexual abuse.
4. To identify the social and family factors that may contribute to abuse and neglect.

Lecture Guidelines:

   I. Recognizing abuse and neglect.
      A. The professional's role in recognizing abuse.
         1. Law enforcement personnel may be first on the scene

of a reported domestic call.
2. A professional's observations can be an important contribution to the protection of children.
3. The professional should be aware that someone other than the parent may have inflicted the abuse: a sibling, a relative, or a caretaker.
4. The professional's evaluation may be critical to the child's safety.

II. The professional's on-the-scene observations may be a major source of information.
   A. The professional should note and record.
      1. The physical setting of the home, including eating and cooking facilities, sleeping, heating, and space allocation as well as the general cleanliness or lack of sanitation in the home.
      2. The physical condition of all of the children in the home, including the manner of dress, general appearance and any observable injuries.
      3. The interaction of the parents and children.
      4. The nonverbal communication that confirms or discredits the verbal communication.
      5. Observations of an individual's behavior can serve to confirm or contradict the learner's judgment of the situation.
      6. Evidence of alcohol and drug use.
      7. Subjective observations combined with physical evidence in the event that a court case becomes necessary.

Method of Presentation

The lecture method is used to present material on recognizing signs of abuse and neglect. The topic of the lecture should be introduced by noting the importance of a professional's being aware of child abuse and neglect indicators. Emphasize the importance of the initial interview in which the officer or social worker must be aware of both the characteristics of abusive parents or caretakers and the indicators in the child. This area will be expanded in Module IV which is concerned with intervention and the actual investigative process in cases of child abuse and neglect.

The blackboard will be used to reinforce the main ideas of the lecture. The learners will be asked to list the observable factors that they can recall from the lecture. The learners' suggestions and ideas will then be used to expand the list in order to relate the newly-presented material of the lecture to the learners' experiences.

In this session, the role-playing is suggested as a method for encouraging group participation and for reinforcing the material presented in the lecture. The trainer should be familiar with role-playing and feel confident with its use. The following role-play profile is designed to give the learners practice in recognizing and recording, at the scene, physical and behavioral indicators of child abuse and neglect. Four learners will be assigned to a group. Each one will assume the role of either the mother, father, child, or officer. Each person is given a role profile. The learners will rehearse their role for five minutes. The remainder of the group will observe the scene and will participate in a discussion of the role-play scene.

Resource Material: Role-Profile 1

A police officer arrives on the scene of a domestic call. As he approaches the door, the shouting lessens, he is allowed to enter, and he finds the father, mother, and child.

The father is big, strong, loud, unkempt, and irritated.

The mother, of average build, is visibly shaken, bothered by the intrusion, but cooperative.

The child, a 5-year-old boy, cowering in a corner, seems terrified of the intruder in uniform, but he cannot hide his considerable pain.

Discussion Questions:

1. What should the professional look for?
2. Was the behavior of the parents consistent with their story?
3. What details of the physical setting either confirmed or discredited their story?
4. What more could the learner doing the role-playing have done, recorded or observed?

Session 2: Physical Indicators of Child Abuse and Neglect

This session is primarily concerned with the physical indicators of child abuse and neglect that have been drawn from a variety of sources. Physical abuse of children includes any nonaccidental injury caused by the child's parent or caretakers: burning, beating, branding, punching, etc. By definition, the injury is not an accident; however, the intent of the caretaker may not have been to injure the child. Physical abuse may not be intentional, but the result of over-discipline or other punishment inappropriate to the child's age or condition. Accidents do cause many childhood injuries. Although they may sound extreme, the indicators listed do happen, and they must be understood and reported. The repeated occurrence of an indicator, or the presence of several indicators in combination, or the appearance of serious injury or suspicious death should alert the professional to the possibility of child abuse and/or neglect.

Content Material: Lecture Guidelines

I. Physical Abuse
  A. Physical indicators of abuse in the child.
    1. Unexplained bruises and welts on the face, lips, and mouth.
    2. Evidence of malnutrition or failure-to-thrive.
    3. Fractures and lacerations.
    4. Burns.
    5. Evidence of overall poor care.
    6. Poor motor development.
    7. Head injuries.
    8. Has been given inappropriate food, drink, or drugs.
    9. Bruises in various stages of healing.
    10. Bruises on the large areas of the body, the back, buttocks, or thighs.
    11. Bruises in clusters or patterns that could indicate the article used to inflict the wound: i.e., belt, cord, buckle.
    12. Bruises on different surfaces indicating the blows came from different directions.

II. Neglect
   A. Physical indicators of neglect in the child.
      1. Evidence of poor hygiene.
      2. Evidence of repeated injury.
      3. Unexplained abdominal injury.
         a. Swelling of the abdomen.
         b. Localized tenderness.
         c. Frequent vomiting.
      4. Human bite marks.
      5. Constant hunger.
      6. Inappropriate clothing.
      7. Constant lack of supervision, especially when engaged in dangerous activities and for extended periods of time.
      8. Constant fatigue or listlessness.
      9. Unattended physical problems or medical needs.

Method of Presentation

During this session, the lecture and discussion methods are used to present the physical indicators of abuse and neglect found in children. A discussion of the indicators should follow the lecture. This listing is not intended to be exhaustive, moreover, a single incident may not indicate abuse, but the presence of several indicators or incidents should alert the learner to suspect child abuse and/or neglect.

The lecture will emphasize that angry feelings about such conditions must be channeled into appropriate action to help the abused child. Questions, comments, and discussion from the group should be encouraged during as well as after the lecture. A review of the discussion of attitudes and how they may affect the performance of one's duty will be appropriate in this context.

Session 3: Behavioral Indicators of Abuse and Neglect

This session will explore the behavioral indicators that may be used in identifying cases of child abuse and neglect. In the previous session, the more obvious physical signs of abuse and/or neglect were discussed. However, less obvious, almost indiscernable behavioral indicators of abuse are also important for the learner in identifying abuse. In addition to the areas of behavior in children, a list of behaviors to watch for in parents and caretakers will be presented for discussion. The frequency and consistency of these indicators should be noted.

Content Material: Lecture Guidelines

I. Abuse
   A. Behavioral indicators of abuse in children.
      1. Actions as well as physical signs can be an indicator of abuse in children.
      2. Abused and neglected children may display certain characteristics which should be recognizable to the sensitive professional.
      3. In adolescents, behavior may be the only clue to abuse and neglect, because they may have learned to hide the physical signs.
      4. A child wary of physical contact with adults may shrink at their approach.
      5. A child may become frightened at the sound of other children crying.
      6. A child may seem frightened of his parents.
      7. A child may talk or show signs of having been injured by a parent.

II. Neglect
   A. The behavioral indicators of neglect differ because of the very nature of the offense.
      1. Neglect involves a lack of attention to the basic needs of a child, including food, clothing, shelter, medical care, and supervision.
      2. Physical abuse tends to occur sporadically, while neglect tends to be chronic; therefore, the frequency of indicators is more important in neglect cases.
   B. Behavioral indicators of neglect found in children.
      1. A child may beg or steal to get food.
      2. A child may often fall asleep in class.
      3. A child may rarely attend school.

4. A child may arrive at school late and leave early.

5. A child may show signs of drug or alcohol addiction.

6. A child may engage in acts of vandalism or theft.

7. A child may say that no one cares for or looks after him/her.

8. A child may show signs of overall poor care.

9. A child may be unusually fearful.

10. A child may seem to be taking care of his parents' needs.

11. A child may be seen as different or bad by the parent.

12. A child who is different or handicapped physically or emotionally may be treated badly by parents because of it.

13. A child may be very aggressive.

14. A young child may have inappropriate responses.

15. A child may have poor mental and language development.

16. A child may show signs of apathy and may fail to respond.

Lecture Guidelines:

I. Behavioral indicators of abuse and neglect.

   A. Behavioral indicators of parents.

   1. A parent may degrade or ridicule the child.

   2. A parent may use extreme punishment as a method of discipline.

   3. A parent may have unrealistic expectations of the child.

   4. A parent may fail to provide adequate food, clothing, shelter or medical care for the child.

   5. A parent may have a history of abuse, institutional care, marital stress, and lack of support systems.

   6. A parent may lose control.

   7. A parent may present a contradictory history of the child's injuries.

   8. A parent may seem detached from the child's problems.

   9. A parent may refuse consent for further diagnosis,

refuse to give accurate information, and may seek out
new hospitals when an injury occurs.

10. A parent may be missing.

11. A parent may be psychotic or psychopathic.

Method of Presentation

The lecture method is used in this session to present material on
the behavioral indicators of abuse and neglect that may be observed
in both parents and children. Most of these behavioral indicators of
neglect, in themselves, do not constitute a case of neglect. At one
time or another, concerned parents may be guilty of one or more of
these indicators, so their frequency and consistency are important.
In considering the indicators of neglect, one must consider questions
such as: (1) How frequently do the indicators occur? (2) What are
the circumstances surrounding the indicators? (3) In the child's
neighborhood, do all of the children display these indicators or only
a few? (4) Is the behavior indicative of true neglect or just a different
life-style?

A question-and-answer approach will be used to introduce the lecture on behavioral indicators in parents. The group should be asked
to suggest some behavioral indicators of abuse. The suggestions
should be listed on the blackboard and discussed by the group. Many
of the indicators will be suggested by the group. The lecture material
will expand the list and provide additional discussion material. A
summary statement should include time to answer any remaining
questions about the behavioral indicators of children and parents that
were brought out in the lecture and listed on the blackboard.

Session 4: Sexual Abuse and its Indicators

This session will concern itself with sexual abuse of children. As
with the other areas of abuse, definition of terms vary as to specific
language. Some of these definitions will be considered. Sexual abuse
has been generally defined as any contacts or interactions between a
child and an adult in which the child is being used for sexual stimu-
lation. These acts may be considered sexual abuse if committed
against a child by a person who is under eighteen but older than the
victim and in power or control.

The emotional affects on children of some police intervention procedures in investigating cases of sexual abuse are explored. Module IV will stress intervention and investigation techniques more fully in order for the learner to correlate the learning experiences of the current session with those in later sessions.

Some general information about sexual abuse will be followed by more specific information concerning the physical indicators of sexual abuse. Because a child's safety is involved in child abuse and neglect cases, the professional must be alert to the signals of child abuse and neglect. Most state laws require the reporting of suspected abuse, knowledge of these indicators insures that an informed decision will be made.

Content Material: Lecture Guidelines

I. Sexual Abuse.
- A. Definition
  1. Sexual exploitation of children has been defined as the involvement of dependent and immature children and adolescents in sexual activities for which they are unable to give informed consent.

II. Incest
- A. Incest is a common form of sexual abuse.
  1. Sexual abuse frequently occurs between the child and someone familiar to him or her.
  2. Incest may be violent or nonviolent sexual intercourse between family members.
  3. Acting-out adolescent girls may be suffering from both physical abuse and sexual molestation.
  4. The mother may be aware of the incest and do nothing about it.

III. Socioeconomic aspects of incest.
- A. The social, medical, and criminal justice systems tend to handle middle and upper class fathers in a different manner.
  1. The majority of fathers convicted of incest with their daughters were of a low socioeconomic background.
  2. Those people from the lower socioeconomic groups

and/or minorities are more visible, more likely to be found out.

3. Such people are more likely to require the aid of social service agencies.

4. Such people are more likely to be charged and convicted.

Lecture Guidelines:

I. Indicators of sexual abuse.
   A. Physical signs of sexual abuse of children.
      1. The child may have difficulty in walking or sitting.
      2. The child may have torn, stained, or bloody under clothing.
      3. The child may complain of pain or itching in the genital area.
      4. The child may have bruises or bleeding in external genital areas.
      5. A report may be made of venereal disease, particularly in a child under thirteen.
      6. Pregnancy may occur in early adolescence.
   B. Behavioral indicators.
      1. The child may appear withdrawn.
      2. The child may engage in fantasy or infantile behavior and appear retarded.
      3. The child may have poor peer relationships.
      4. The child may be unwilling to participate in physical activities.
      5. The child may engage in delinquent acts or run away.
      6. The child may display bizarre sexual behavior or unusual sexual knowledge.
      7. The child may admit sexual assault by a caretaker.
      8. An adolescent female may act out sexually in response to sexual molestation.

Method of Presentation

In this session, the lecture method is used to explore a variety of aspects of sexual abuse. The lecture-discussion method will be used to present information and get feed-back from the learners about the facts and myths of sexual abuse.

Because sexual abuse is a highly emotional topic, the discussion will include some elements related to the prevailing attitudes toward sexual abuse. In order to reveal the feelings concerning the topic of sexual abuse, some cases will be introduced that were designed to review the attitudes of the learners.

Cases 2 and 3 have been provided for the trainer. The cases and the accompanying discussion questions may be expanded by the trainer to meet the specific needs of the group. In the discussion which follows the cases, the learners may include either actual or hypothetical cases. The trainer should note that the investigation and intervention process will be examined at length in Module IV.

Resource Material:

Case #2:

Officer Carol Jones arrived at the home of the Johnsons to answer a call about a runaway teen. While obtaining a description of the Johnson's missing 15-year-old daughter, Officer Jones didn't think that this home environment would make a 15 year old want to leave. Her father seemed convinced that Susan had run away. Her mother said that Susan had been showing signs of stress, related to school work. Mrs. Johnson thought that Susan must have had an accident as she could think of nothing that would cause her daughter to run away.

Officer Jones filed the report, but she couldn't file away some of the impressions she had about the Johnson family. She couldn't be specific, but her instincts told her that something was wrong in the Johnson family. Mr. Johnson was a successful businessman; Mrs. Johnson was a school teacher. Susan was a better than average student who had been missing for three days.

When Officer Jones got the call that Susan had been found, she had an opportunity to talk to Susan. Susan was eager to talk to Officer Jones. She told of an incestuous relationship with her father that had frightened her and had caused her to run away. At first she valued the close affectionate relationship with her father, but as her father demanded more and more of her, she felt shame, guilt, and fear. She felt fear of discovery, fear of her father's threats to expose her to her friends, and fear of her father's anger. In a desperate situation, she wanted to run away as far and fast as she could.

Discussion Questions: Case 2

1. Considering the family's socioeconomic background, should Officer Jones return Susan to her home and hope that the Johnsons may seek professional help?
2. Should Officer Jones call a social agency in on the case prior to returning Susan to her parents' home?
3. Should Susan be taken to a family treatment center instead of being returned home?
4. What values and beliefs do you think would cause you to take the action you select?

The students should be given an opportunity to consider alternative ways of handling the situation; their beliefs and values must be translated into behaviors and actions.

Case #3:

Officers Wilson and Olsen arrived on the scene of a domestic call in a very low socioeconomic neighborhood. When Mrs. Lee let them in, she explained that she came home from work early and found her husband sexually molesting her daughter. He eight-year-old daughter was screaming in terror. Her husband quivered and cried like a cornered animal. Mr. Lee was pleading for help and apologizing for what had taken place. Both he and the child said it had never happened before.

Discussion Questions: Case 3

1. What action should the officer take?
2. Who should be the officers first concern?
3. How do you think the officers are feeling about the scene?
4. Might the officers feelings, beliefs, and values enter into their decision concerning action?

Resources: Required for the Instructor as Background for Teaching Module III

1. Broadhurst, P.P., and Knoeller, J.S., *The Role of Law Enforcement in the Prevention and Treatment of Child Abuse and Neglect*. National Cen-

ter on Child Abuse and Neglect, Administration for Children, Youth and Families Children's Bureau. Office of Human Development, U.S. Dept. of Health and Human Services, Aug. 1979.

This publication contains information which directly links the role and responsibility of law enforcement personnel to the protection of children in society.

2. Eberling, N.B., and Hill, D.A. (Eds.), *Child Abuse: Intervention and Treatment*. Aeton: Publishing Sciences Group Inc., 1975.

The contributors to this book include professionals from many disciplines involved in cases of abuse and neglect. It contains insight into the social and economic factors involved in both the reported and nonreported cases of abuse and neglect.

3. Green, F.C., Introduction: Child Sexual Abuse, *Pediatric Ann.* 8(5) May, 1979.

This article by Dr. Green will serve as an informative introduction to the area of child sexual abuse.

4. Kempe, C.H. and Helfer, R.E. (Eds.), *Helping the Battered Child and His Family*. Philadelphia: Lippincott Company, 1972.

This book defines and describes the various categories of abuse and suggests an approach to the identification, prevention, and treatment of abusive families.

5. U.S. Department of Health and Human Services. *Child Sexual Abuse: Incest, Assault, and Sexual Exploitation*. Administration for Children. Youth and Families Childrens' Bureau. National Center on Child Abuse and Neglect, April, 1981.

This publication provides an overview of recent research findings concerning the nature, extent, dynamics and effects of child sexual abuse as well as some identification and treatment techniques.

CHAPTER 4

MODULE IV — INTERVENTION AND INVESTIGATION OF CHILD ABUSE AND NEGLECT

MODULE OVERVIEW

INTERVENTION and investigation involve both fact gathering and appropriate case disposition. The job of the investigator is examined: receiving the report, protecting the child, gathering evidence of abuse and neglect, interviewing the parent, interviewing the child, and interviewing witnesses. Appropriate disposition alternative are also examined.

In most jurisdictions, the Child Protective Services Unit is the key agency in the community's child abuse and neglect response system. It has the legally-mandated responsibility for the preventive, investigative, evaluative, and treatment programs. Law enforcement plays a supportive role to that of Child Protective Services. All professionals should be aware of Child Protective Services role in abuse and neglect cases. Law enforcement officers all over the country are becoming part of a team of professionals which includes educators, social workers, and health-related professionals who work with a variety of agencies to provide efficient, effective case handling.

Module IV focuses on the role of law enforcement in cases of physical and sexual abuse of children. However, the techniques of information gathering, observation reporting, and interviewing are relevant to all professionals who deal with children and are required by law to report suspected cases of abuse.

Objectives

1. To increase the trainees' awareness of the appropriate intervention procedures in answering a report of child abuse or neglect.
2. To apply appropriate information-gathering techniques to a child abuse or neglect investigation.
3. To utilize police power according to the law and with knowledgeable discretion.
4. To identify the necessary information about gathering and evaluating evidence in child abuse and neglect cases.
5. To apply effective interviewing techniques with both children and adults involved.
6. To be familiar with all applicable disposition alternatives.

Schedule:

Session 1: Intervention
Session 2: Investigation
Session 3: Gathering Evidence and Case Disposition

Session 1: Intervention

During the first session of Module IV, an introduction and an overview of child abuse and neglect intervention and investigative procedures will be presented. A discussion of module objectives will familiarize the learners with the areas to be covered and give some direction and continuity to the sequence of sessions in the module. This module focuses on the areas of child abuse and neglect which directly involve personnel in the investigation, intervention, and disposition of abuse and neglect cases. Session one concentrates on the intervention process that begins with an initial report of abuse or family disturbance.

Content Material: Discuss Module Objectives

Preliminary Discussion Questions:

1. From what sources might an agency receive a report of abuse or neglect?
2. For what reasons might it be important to approach the person making the report with sensitivity and a supportive attitude?

3. Why would it be important to assure the person making the report that his identity would be kept confidential?
4. What kind of information should the professional attempt to obtain? Why?
5. What kinds of observations should the professional be making?
6. What information should he obtain about the incident which precipitated the report?

Lecture Guidelines:

I. Reports of abuse and/or neglect.
   A. A report may be received from one of a number of sources.
      1. A hospital staff person.
      2. A teacher or other professional.
      3. A police dispatcher.
      4. A neighbor or friend.
      5. A family member.
      6. The report may be made to the police officer on the phone, by a police radio dispatcher, or in person.
   B. The professional may need to interview the person making the report in the field.
      1. He must support and reassure the reporter.
      2. He must convey his understanding of the difficulties involved in making a report.
   C. He should assure the reporter that he is protected.
      1. By immunity from prosecution in the event of an honest mistake.
      2. By his identification being kept confidential.
   D. Reporting suspected child abuse and/or neglect may be difficult for a person.
      1. The reporter usually has considered the consequences to the child as well as the entire family.
      2. The prospective reporter may decide it easier not to report.
      3. The prospective reporter probably has realized that his report may result in the removal of the child from the family.

4. The reporter may have difficulty convincing himself that his call can help the family rather than hurt it.

II. Social and cultural factors.
  A. Many social and cultural factors influence a citizen's decision to report abuse.
    1. Society feels strongly about family privacy.
    2. Society feels discipline and the treatment of children are the responsibility of parents.
    3. Society has only recently started to recognize children's rights, at home and in the courtroom.
    4. Many segments of society still believe strongly that parents are best suited to raise a child and that keeping intact the family unit is of the highest priority.

III. Personal Factors
  A. Personal considerations can affect a person's willingness to report suspected neglect and/or abuse.
    1. A strong deterrent to reporting is the reluctance of an individual to get involved in other people's lives.
    2. Apathy may result in an individual not getting involved.
    3. An individual may be ignorant about the protection a reporter receives.
    4. An individual may fear reprisal by the abuser involved.
    5. An individual may fear becoming involved in a process about which he may be uniformed.
    6. An individual may fear involving the police or other authority figures in a family matter.
    7. An individual may fear that his misinterpretation of the facts may have resulted in an inappropriate conclusion.

Method of Presentation

Initially, a class discussion of this topic will be used by the instructor to determine the group's previous learning levels. For this discussion, the group will be divided into smaller groups of four or five members. Each group will be given one of the preliminary discussion questions provided in the content section. A recorder should be selected in each of the groups to take notes on the group's combined answer to the question. The reporter will present their findings to the entire group for their comments and consideration.

This discussion prior to the presentation of the lecture information will indicate to the instructor the group's level of previous learning. The trainer should be familiar with the technique of small and large group discussion before using this method of presentation. The lecture method will be used to provide the knowledge and background information regarding the receipt of an initial report of abuse.

To summarize the lecture, the trainer should ask how they feel about making reports. These feelings should be explored in an understanding way by the group. Many professionals are required by law to report suspected cases of abuse and neglect. Therefore, they must understand the importance of the law as it concerns the health and safety of children. The greater their understanding of the law and of their feelings, the more skilled they will become in the enormous task of protecting children.

It is important for professionals of all disciplines to be familiar with the process of investigating cases of physical and sexual abuse in order to better understand their individual role in the context of the broader spectrum.

Knowledge of law enforcement's role in abuse cases will encourage the interdisciplinary cooperation and understanding needed to successfully adjudicate these cases. Act 124 will be further explored in Module V.

A closing statement should lead into the following session which will cover investigative procedures in cases of abuse and neglect.

Session 2: Investigation

In this session, the investigative tools of general police work are applied to cases of child abuse and neglect. The traditional areas of police work and police expertise, such as investigation and the discovery of evidence, are related to child abuse and neglect. Traditional criminal investigations and child abuse investigations will be contrasted. The difference emphasized throughout this session is that the focus of most investigations is on the prosecution of the perpetrator; in abuse cases, the focus is on the protection of the child. Appropriate interviewing procedures will be discussed for parents, children, and witnesses.

The previous session outlined the many ways in which a report of suspected abuse or neglect may reach an agency. When a report is received the investigation begins.

Content Material: Lecture Guidelines

I. Receipt of a report.
   A. Having obtained a report of suspected neglect and/or abuse, the professional should collect several types of information.
      1. Identifying information, i.e., name, address, age, and sex of the child involved and the date and time of the incident.
      2. The present location of the child as well as where the incident occurred.
      3. The name and address of the person or institution responsible for the child.
      4. The name and address of the alleged abuser.
      5. The names of other persons living in the home.
      6. The nature of the suspected abuse or neglect and any information on previous injury to the child or any siblings.
      7. The status of the case to this point.
      8. The reporter's name, address and phone number, if he has permission to use it.
      9. The relationship of the reporter to the family.
      10. The willingness of the reporter to participate in the case.
      11. The motives of the reporter.
      12. The location of possible witnesses to the incident.
   B. A routine record check of the family should be done to determine.
      1. Prior reports of suspected child abuse and neglect.
      2. Services already being provided because of a previous report.

II. Police Role

    A. The primary concern of the law enforcement officer in cases of neglect and abuse is the protection of the child. The investigator must determine:

       1. Is the child abuse or neglect actually occurring?

       2. Is the child at risk in the home?

       3. Is immediate intervention necessary for the child's safety?

    Once these questions have been answered, the investigator must determine.

       4. Whether further police involvement is indicated.

       5. Whether the case should be referred to Children and Youth Services or some other agency better able to handle the problem.

       6. Whether the case is a false report with no further action indicated.

III. Right of entry into the home.

The officer's entry into the home will depend on the circumstances. If the officers demonstrate concern and sympathy, and if they explain their role in ensuring the safety of the child, they are likely to gain entry. In some cases, the police will be seen as intruders, treated with anger and hostility, and not allowed in.

    A. In every state, the officer will have the right of forcible entry if:

       1. He has probable cause to believe a child in the home is in imminent danger.

       2. He has probable cause to believe that a crime is being committed in the home.

    B. If the police are denied entry, and the situation is not an emergency, a court order or search warrant is advisable.

Lecture Guidelines:

I. Interviewing parents.

    A. Interviewing the parents may be the most important step in the investigation. Due process rights granted by the fourth and fifth amendments to the constitution must be observed.

1. The fourth concerns "unreasonable searches and seizures."
2. The fifth concerns self-incrimination.
3. Miranda rights must be made known or voluntarily waived.

II. Interview setting.
   1. The parents should be interviewed separately.
   2. The interview should be in private as comfortable an environment as possible to get the needed information.
   3. The interview should be conducted in a professional nonjudgmental manner.

III. Interview techniques.
   A. The investigator should consider how his actions will impact on the family; anger will be met with anger.
      1. He can appear understanding to the parent without appearing approving.
      2. Child abuse and neglect can make an investigator angry, but the trained officer will realize that these feelings may impair professional judgment.
      3. An attempt to coerce a confession may make a future treatment relationship difficult to establish.

Blackboard Chart. During an interview with parents an investigator should:
   A. Observe the due process rights granted by the 4th and 5th Amendments.
   B. Conduct the interview in private.
   C. Explain the reason for the interview.
   D. Be sympathetic, understanding, and professional.

During an interview with parents, an officer should not:
   A. Try to "prove" abuse or neglect by anger or accusations.
   B. Show outward signs of anger or disapproval of the child, parent, or situation.
   C. Verbalize judgments or place blame concerning the situation.
   D. Pry into family matters unrelated to the situation at hand.
   E. Reveal the source of a report.

Lecture Guidelines:

I. Techniques for interviewing the child.
   A. At times, a child must be interviewed initially in order to learn what has happened. Every attempt should be made to avoid the need for the child-victim interview. Specially-trained personnel should be available to do the interview.
      1. The purpose of the initial interview with the child is to verify the report.
      2. Initial contact with the child will help determine whether the child is in imminent danger.

II. Decision to interview.
   A. The decision to interview a child or not, depends on several factors:
      1. The child's age and condition.
      2. The child's ability to evaluate or relate what has happened.
      3. The possible impact of the interview on the child.
      4. The permission of the parents for the interview.
      5. The possibility of retaliation by the parents, if they strongly object.
      6. The precautions to insure that the parents will not retaliate against the child.

III. Interview setting.
   A. The interview may take place in a variety of settings:
      1. Medical facility
      2. School
      3. Child Care Center
      4. Home

IV. Interview attitude and atmosphere.
   A. When interviewing the child concerning possible abuse or conditions of neglect, the interviewer should remember that the child may be hurt, in pain, fearful, confused, etc.
      1. The child should be made as comfortable as possible whatever the circumstances.
      2. Children should be assured that they are not in trouble and are not at fault.
      3. Interviewing children in cases of sexual assualt calls for

extreme sensitivity and skill.

4. In addition to feelings of fear and confusion, they may feel blame and guilt.

5. Understanding and reassurance may be communicated to the child more easily if the interviewer is the same sex as the child.

V. Techniques for the interviewer.
   A. The interviewer should be sensitive to the situation.
      1. The interviewer must try to determine the emotional state of the child.
      2. The interviewer should attempt to gain the child's confidence with a friendly demeanor.
      3. The investigator should remain calm and neutral upon hearing the facts.
      4. The interview should be conducted in language the child can comprehend. In cases of sexual abuse, terms need to be explained to identify the offense. In some states, the police have used anatomically correct dolls to help young children tell about the incident.
      5. Children should be permitted to relate the incident in their own way.
      6. If the child is an adolescent and in need of supervision, the officer may feel a need for a petition. If so, the child should be informed of his Miranda Rights.

Blackboard Chart. During an interview with a child, an investigator should:
   A. Build a feeling of trust in the child.
   B. Conduct the interview in private.
   C. Explain to the child how the information will be used.
   D. Use language the child can understand.
   E. Explain his need to see the child's injuries in a comforting manner.
   F. Try to explain to the child what will happen next.

During an interview with a child, an investigator should not:
   A. Make the child feel in trouble or at fault.
   B. Criticize the child's words.
   C. Lead the child to answer in a certain way.
   D. Pressure the child for answers.

    E. Display horror, shock, or disapproval of the parents or the situation.

    F. Force the child to remove clothing to show bruises.

    G. Conduct the interview in a group.

Lecture Guidelines:

I. Techniques for interviewing witnesses.

    A. Witnesses to abuse are rare, since most incidents occur within the privacy of the home.

        1. Witnesses may be helpful to corroborate evidence of a child's condition and home situation:

           a. Teachers

           b. Siblings

           c. Relatives

           d. Neighbors

           e. Family physician

    B. An investigator should remember that witnesses may be reluctant to discuss a family crisis with an outsider because:

        1. They fear retaliation by the family.

        2. They fear it would violate a confidence.

        3. They fear becoming involved.

Method of Presentation

In this session, the trainer should select the training materials that best suit the needs of the group, the training objectives, and the time available for presentation. The trainer should employ those methods with which he or she is most familiar and confident. The material is presented by the use of lectures, blackboard charts, small and large group discussion, and the case study techniques.

The lecture method is used to present new information. To summarize the important points made in the lectures on interviewing children and parents, examples should be elicited from the group and listed on the chalkboard.

Group discussion, small group techniques, and the case method will then be used to review and reinforce the information in the lectures. The case studies presented in this session are designed and structured to enable the learner to apply the cognitive information in simulated situations. The cases deal with police-related interactions and will enable the learner to relate the new information to his experiences.

Interviewing parents and children in cases of abuse and neglect is extremely important to the resolution of the family's crisis situation. The initial interview can have emotional and psychological implications regarding future treatment for the family. For this reason, a guest lecturer from the field of psychology or social services would aid in the presentation of this material. Such a person would lend expertise to the material and familiarize police personnel with another discipline's handling of child abuse and neglect cases. The importance of working well with a variety of disciplines will be further explored in Module VI and Module VII.

Resource Material:

Case Study 4:

The following case study is designed to provoke thought and discussion about the information presented in the lectures. The discussion questions are designed to review and reinforce the lecture information and apply it to practical situations.

Case Study 4, Part 1:

At 10:24 P.M., on January 23, juvenile officers, Jim Taylor and Ann Reed, received a radio call in response to an anonymous phone call to the police department. The caller said that a Mrs. Lila White, at 13103 Webster Avenue, was drunk and beating her daughter. The caller added that she had reported past instances of abuse to Child and Youth Services. To the caller's knowledge, that department's only response was to have a social worker visit the house.

Discussion Questions for Part 1:

1. What information should officers Taylor and Reed try to obtain before the initial contact?
2. What effect does the reporter's request for anonymity have on the investigation? On the validity of the call? On the way in which

the officer's approach the call?
3. What should be the primary consideration of the officers in answering this call?
4. What attitudes and feelings may have to be dealt with?

Case Study 4, Part 2:

Officers Taylor and Reed went to the scene to make their investigation and interview Mrs. White. At 10:30 P.M., the officers had to knock several times before Mrs. White appeared at the door with a crying little girl clutching to her skirt. The officers explained that they were investigating a complaint that a child was in danger, and they asked to come in. Entering, the officers observed a very dirty apartment. The living room floor was covered with garbage and empty liquor bottles. Mrs. White was angry, hostile, and drunk. The child appeared to be about four years old and seemed relieved to see the officers. The child was dirty and dressed in filthy underwear. They saw fresh bruises on the child's exposed arms and legs as well as other bruises in various stages of healing.

Discussion Questions, Part 2:

1. What observations should the officer note?
2. How should the officers approach Mrs. White?
3. How should the officers approach the child?
4. What kind of information should the officers seek from Mrs. White?
5. What records should the officers check?

Session 3: Gathering Evidence and Case Disposition

This session explores the investigative process that deals specifically with aspects of evidence gathering and case disposition. Many possible case dispositions and their applications are examined. The information presented in this session is an outgrowth and follow-up of the instruction of the previous session. It will review the previous session, while the previous session will lay the ground work for the current session. This continuity is designed to facilitate the learning process.

Content Material: Lecture Guidelines

I. Gathering techniques.
  A. Gathering evidence in a child abuse or neglect case can be very difficult.
    1. The parents may be hostile and aggressive.
    2. The parents may be silent and withdrawn.
    3. The children may be too young, too frightened, or unwilling to talk to the investigator.
    4. Other witnesses, friends, or neighbors may be unwilling to interfere in a family problem.
    5. The circumstances may be clear to the investigator, but the act or omission may or may not constitute abuse or neglect.

II. Evidence gathering in cases of abuse and neglect is similar to that used in other kinds of cases.
  A. The four methods of collecting evidence are:
    1. Interviews.
    2. Documenting or photographing observations.
    3. Searching relevant records and files.
    4. Identifying and collecting physical evidence.

III. Involved professionals.
  A. Law enforcement officers should be aware of the contribution of other professions to the case of abuse and neglect.
    1. Interviews with medical personnel to obtain evidence concerning the child's injuries or poor health may be needed.
    2. Interviews with social workers, psychologists, and health-related professionals may be necessary.

IV. Observation is an integral part of the interview process.
  A. The investigator should record his observations accurately and in detail. Notes should be recorded about.
    1. The physical condition of all the children, including their general appearance, health, and injuries.
    2. The health and safety of the environment.
    3. The general condition of the home, including availability and adequacy of food, water, heat, light, and space.

B. Experienced and knowledgeable officers should observe and record the behavior of parents and children, including:
   1. Their reaction to the officer.
   2. The pattern of interaction within the family.
   3. Emotional stability.
   4. The presence or absence of communication.

V. Photographs as evidence.
   A. Photographs are an important form of evidence. Often they are the best way to record observable child abuse and neglect involving serious injury and neglectful home conditions.
      1. Photographs should be taken as soon as possible, before bruises and contusions heal and disappear.
      2. Most photographs and/or x-rays are done in hospitals or doctors' offices while the child is being treated.
      3. As with evidence in all cases, the photographs·should be properly marked and handled.
      4. The officer should be certain to instruct the photographer about the special needs òf an abused or neglected child. The child may already be upset, and care should be taken to prevent further alarm.
      5. Photographs of the home can be used to document filth, exposed wiring, or inadequate plumbing.

VI. Physical evidence.
   A. The officers should collect physical evidence as soon as possible. Physical evidence may include:
      1. The instrument that was used to inflict the injury.
      2. Guns or poison found within the reach of unsupervised children.
      3. In cases of sexual abuse, most physical evidence is obtained from laboratory tests or physical examination.
   B. Evidence of sexual abuse might include:
      1. Hair samples.
      2. Blood on clothing of suspect or victim.
      3. Semen on the mouth, genitalia, or clothing of the victim.

    4. Fingerprints on implements or weapons used by the abuser.
  C. When obtaining evidence for laboratory examination from a suspect, the proper legal procedures must be followed as in any other case.
    1. Miranda warnings.
    2. Search warrant.
VII. Records check.
  A. In investigating and evaluating reports of suspected abuse and neglect, records searches are important. In addition to providing valuable background information, the records check may identify any agency or childcare professionals who are working with the family. A records check can provide information on which to base an appropriate disposition decision. A check on the reported family, if time permits, prior to responding to the report should include:
    1. Internal police department files.
    2. State wide police records.
    3. Records from the juvenile court.

Lecture Guidelines:

  I. Case disposition.
  A. Law enforcement disposition of child abuse and neglect cases may range from temporary measures to more permanent ones:
    1. Taking the child into protective custody.
    2. Referral to Children and Youth Services for treatment.
    3. Arrest of the parent.
    4. Referrel to court for judicial action.
  II. Disposition alternatives.
  A. Protective custody.
    1. In cases of child abuse and neglect, the law enforcement officer should remember that the first priority is the protection of the child.
    2. In a case of clear and present danger, the child may be placed in protective custody to ensure the child's

safety and well being.

3. Protective custody is a temporary measure, pending arrangements for long-term treatment of the family or prosecution of the caretakers responsible for the abuse and neglect.

4. In all states, law enforcement officers have the right to place a child in protective custody in cases of imminent danger to the child if he were to remain in the custody of parents or caretakers.

5. A police officer may detain a child in:
   a. A medical facility.
   b. An emergency foster home.
   c. A juvenile shelter.

6. When protective custody is exercised, the caretaker should receive written notice of this action and be advised of his legal rights.

7. All states require that a child abuse and neglect petition be filed in Juvenile court within 24 hours of the protective custody.

8. A custody hearing must be held soon after to review the custody status. This review determines if protective custody will continue pending an adjudicatory hearing or will be revoked with the child returning home.

9. A decision to remove a child from his parent or caretaker should be made in conjunction with the chief juvenile officer, Children and Youth Services, and with medical approval and cooperation.

10. Close cooperation between disciplines is necessary for the protection of children. This point will be developed in Module VI and VII.

B. Concerning the possibility of protective custody, an officer should consider these conditions:

1. The present or potential for maltreatment is such that a child may suffer permanent damage to mind or body if not removed.

2. The parents refusal to give the child medical or psychiatric care that the child needs immediately.

3. The child's physical and/or emotional damage indicates that the child needs a supportive place to recuperate.
4. The child is incapable of self-protection.
5. Evidence suggests that the parents are torturing the child or using excessive physical force in the name of discipline.
6. Physical environment of the home creates an immediate threat to the child.
7. Evidence suggests that parental anger will result in severe retaliation against the child.
8. Evidence suggests that the parents are so out of touch with reality that they can't provide for the child's basic needs.
9. The family has a history of hiding the child from outsiders.
10. The family has a history of prior incidents or allegations of abuse.
11. Parent or caretakers have abandoned the child.

C. Other important considerations for the investigator might be:
1. Protection of the child.
2. Personal liability may result from leaving the child alone in a dangerous situation or with a caretaker incapable of caring for the child.
3. Officers should be wary of unofficially placing the children with neighbors or relatives.

III. Referring to a Social Service Agency.
A. The most widely used disposition alternative for child abuse and neglect cases is referral to Children and Youth Services or other appropriate social service agencies.
1. Child abuse and neglect is complex and treatment may be long-term.
2. Treatment may involve a variety of services and programs.
3. Children and Youth Services is best equipped to handle these services and programs.
4. Children and Youth Services is the key agency legally

mandated to handle cases of abuse and neglect in most states.

5. Only in the most serious cases is further police or court action considered.

6. Referral to Children and Youth Services should be made after consultation with the agency and upon agreement with the parents.

7. Final disposition will be made when the social service agency agrees to take the case.

IV. Arrest

A. Arrest of the parents or caretakers in cases of child abuse and/or neglect is the exception, not the rule.

1. Only a small number of cases result in arrest.

2. Arrest may lead to prosecution which is not the best means of dealing with a parent.

3. Changing the parent's behavior is considered the best solution.

4. The aim is not to punish the parent but to protect the child while helping the parents to change.

5. Prosecution can be difficult in all but the most serious cases.

6. Unsuccessful prosecution may increase the risk to the child.

7. Immediate arrest is indicated when the incident is severe.

8. Arrest may be delayed pending consultation with the Children and Youth Services and medical personnel.

B. Arrest may be indicated when:

1. Injury to the child is extremely severe.

2. Evidence exists that a serious crime has been committed.

3. The caretaker may flee jurisdiction.

4. Arrest is necessary to keep the peace.

5. The abuser poses an immediate danger to others.

V. Court Referral.

A. In cases of court intervention, juvenile court is most often used. Criminal prosecution is uncommon in child abuse and neglect cases.

1. Juvenile court provides a coercive but nonpunitive authority to function with Children and Youth Services.
2. This proceeding may persuade the parents to cooperate.

B. Juvenile Courts.
1. Order services for the abusive family.
2. Protect a child from further injury.
3. Provide a forum for a fair and impartial review of agency decisions.
4. Protect the consitutional rights of parents and child.
5. Free the child for adoption and placement in a permanent, safe environment in cases where the parents have been proven unable to care for their child.

C. Criminal prosecution is appropriate only in cases where injury to the child has been severe or where parents are unwilling to protect the child.
1. When a crime such as homicide has resulted from abuse or neglect, criminal prosecution may be the only possible disposition.

D. Referral for criminal prosecution should be considered only in the most severe and serious cases and after consultations with child protective services and other involved professionals. When criminal prosecution results in incarceration, it tends to:
1. Divide the family.
2. Reinforce a sense of isolation, hostility, and resentment.
3. Lead to further abuse in the form of retaliation.
4. Fail the family.

Method of Presentation

For this session, extensive lecture material has been provided. The trainer must use that material which most appropriately applies to the specific group of learners for the alloted training time.

A review is recommended for the material on interview techniques previously presented. The new material will be presented by the lecture and discussion method. The role-playing technique will be used to reinforce the learning, to provoke questions, and to apply the information gained to simulated situations. A role-playing profile and discussion questions are provided.

Resource Material:

Role-Play Profile 2:

You are a juvenile officer with a metropolitan police department. At 3:45 P.M., on a Sunday, you receive a call from a Mr. Wilson in reference to a suspected child abuse situation. Mr. Wilson says he is concerned about the three-year-old son of one of his neighbors. This morning he heard loud shouting and then a child's screams coming from the Lucus' house next door to his. Later in the day, he saw Sam outside and saw several welts and bruises on the child. Sam was in a great deal of pain and hardly able to walk or put pressure on his right leg. Mrs. Lucus was reluctant to discuss Sam's injury with Mr. Wilson, and she refused his suggestion that Sam see a doctor. Mrs. Lucus got angry with Mr. Wilson for continuing to ask about Sam's injury and walked away from him.

Mr. Wilson then told of other occasions when he noticed Sam's physical injuries. Whenever he asked Mrs. Lucus or Mr. Lucus, Sam's stepfather, about the injuries, the parents refused to talk about it or merely said Sam was always falling. Mr. Wilson lived by himself and worked during the day, but often he'd heard the parents shouting and noise which indicated fighting, and Sam seemed to be involved in some way. Mr. Wilson didn't have much background information about family, friends, or relatives. He called the police because it was Sunday and he knew of no friends of the Lucus' to call. He was concerned about Sam's leg; it might be broken and need to be set. He knew of no other source of help, and he felt certain Sam needed help.

After first telephoning the Lucus' home and setting up an interview for that afternoon at 4:30 P.M., you have gone to the house and been allowed in by Mr. and Mrs. Lucus. You have asked to see Sam, and his mother carries him into the room. He can't walk on the injured leg, and you see bruises on his arms. Although it is quite warm, Sam appears in jeans that cover his legs. You are about to question Mr. and Mrs. Lucus concerning the injury and the information you have gotten from the reporter.

Several members of the group should be given an opportunity to role-play the officer and Mr. and Mrs. Lucus. After each role-playing interview, the discussion questions should be used to summarized the session.

Role-Playing Discussion:

You are the officer receiving this call. Take five minutes to develop the strategy you will use to approach this situation and to consider an appropriate interview technique.

Discussion Questions:

1. What observations did you note about the physical environment of the home?
2. What observations did you note about the interaction of the family?
3. Do your observations corroborate the circumstances surrounding Sam's injuries?
4. What other professionals should be contacted?
5. What do you think went well with the interview?
6. What could you have done better?
7. How did you feel during the interview?

Resources: Required for the Instructor as Background for Teaching Module IV

1. Bard, M., *The Function of Police in Crisis Intervention and Conflict Management.* U.S. Department of Justice, L.E.A.A. Washington, D.C.: Criminal Justice Associates, Inc., 1975.

This publication outlines the function of law enforcement's role in crisis intervention. It provides background material for handling of sensitive family conflict situations.

2. Broadhurst, P.P., and Knoeller, J.S., *The Role of Law Enforcement in the Prevention and Treatment of Child Abuse and Neglect.* National Center on Child Abuse and Neglect, Administration for Children Youth and Families Children's Bureau. Office of Human Development, U.S. Dept. of Health and Human Services. August, 1979.

This publication will be helpful in clarifying the rationale as well as the role of police personnel in the prevention and handling of child abuse and neglect situations including sensitive intervention and interviewing techniques.

3. Eberling, N.B., and Hill, D.A., (Eds.), *Child Abuse: Intervention and Treatment*. Acton: Publishing Sciences Group, Inc., 1975.

This book consists of a series of articles contributed by a variety of professionals involved in the intervention and disposition of child abuse cases. It refers to the need for interdisciplinary cooperation.

4. Flammang, C.J., *Police Juvenile Enforcement*. Springfield: Charles C Thomas, 1972.

This book highlights differences in the handling of situations involving juveniles. A case is made for the need for more active police involvement in the area of child protection and child advocacy.

5. Ketterman, T., and Kravitz, M., *Police Crisis Intervention*. Washington, D.C., Institute of Law Enforcement and Criminal Justice, U.S. Department of Justice, 1978.

This publication outlines several successful and innovative programs for police in the area of crisis intervention. It stresses the social service approach to a variety of crisis situations including child abuse.

CHAPTER 5

MODULE V — THE LEGAL PARAMETERS OF CHILD ABUSE AND NEGLECT

MODULE OVERVIEW

THIS module presents the rationale for the role of law enforcements in child abuse and neglect cases. The module includes a description of the police officer's responsibilities under the child abuse and neglect reporting laws, the juvenile court laws, and the applicable criminal laws in most states. Moreover, information is given about the social services approach to child abuse and neglect cases as proscribed by Pennsylvania Act 124. Although the specifics of various state laws may vary, Act 124 represents the kind of child abuse legislation found in all 50 states.

This module presents the legal parameters of child abuse and neglect for police personnel. Because of the specialized nature of the material, an attorney or an instructor with a law or legal background should present the material. An attorney would be familiar with the kinds of cases with which the officers would be confronted. He would have a working knowledge of the court system and the current court decisions that would shed light on the disposition process in cases of abuse and neglect. An attorney would bring a different facet of child abuse and neglect to the learner's attention. He would provide insight into the many legal issues facing the learners when they become involved in cases of abuse and neglect. Such contact between disciplines is necessary for the interdisciplinary cooperation recommended in helping the family in crisis. In the event that a member of the legal profession is not presenting the material, reference materials and lecture guidelines are provided.

Objectives

1. To recognize the reasons surrounding law enforcement involvement in child abuse and neglect.
2. To acquire knowledge of state laws on child abuse and neglect using the Pennsylvania laws as specific examples of state laws in general.
3. To be able to apply the law in child abuse and neglect cases in a nonjudgmental, empathetic manner.
4. To demonstrate a knowledge of relevant child abuse laws and legal processes in cases of abuse and neglect.
5. To acquaint the trainees with the process of reporting and its possible outcomes.

Schedule:

Session 1: Law Enforcement Involvement in Child Abuse and Neglect
Session 2: State Laws Relating to Abuse and Neglect
Session 3: Continuation of Laws Relating to Abuse and Neglect
Session 4: Legal Case Flow

Session 1: Law Enforcement Involvement in Child Abuse and Neglect

The legal parameters of child abuse and neglect for police personnel are presented. The first session begins with an overview of the module content and objectives, then explores the rationale behind law enforcement involvement in child abuse and neglect. In succeeding sessions, the laws which give the police their authority to intervene in child abuse and neglect cases are examined: The Juvenile Act, The Child Protective Services Law, The Adoption Act, and the Protection from Abuse Act. These acts, together with criminal laws that relate to child abuse and neglect, provide the basis for police intervention.

Content Material: Discuss Module Objectives

Lecture Guidelines:

I. Law Enforcement and Child Abuse.
   A. Reasons for involvement of law enforcement officers in the intervention, treatment, and prevention of child abuse and neglect:
      1. Legal mandates exist for law enforcement involvement.
      2. A police officer is a highly-visible helping professional in the community.
      3. An officer has a professional and ethical responsibility.
      4. Law enforcement officers are easily identifiable and readily available around the clock to citizens seeking assistance in a child's behalf. For this reason, the law enforcement agency is often the community resource citizens call upon when child abuse and neglect is discovered.
      5. The law enforcement agency will respond to an emergency situation at most anytime of day or night.
      6. All communities have law enforcement services available to the public.
      7. Law enforcement officers are legally charged with the investigation of murder, mayhem, assault, battery, and sex crimes, even when committed by parents.
      8. Criminal law forbids cruelty to children.
   B. In all states, the role of the police officer is to investigate complaints:
      1. Involving violations of the law.
      2. Involving the preservation of the peace.
      3. Involving the prevention of crime.
   C. In many states, police many take into custody any child who needs protection.
II. The issue of how police are to function.
   A. Criminal sanctions are an ineffective method of preventing child abuse because:
      1. Family crisis situations caused by interlocking stress

factors cannot be controlled or prevented by negative sanctions.

2. A criminal proceeding may punish the victim as well as the offender.
3. A criminal proceeding may do irreparable damage to the family unit.

B. The responsibilities of the law enforcement officer in the child abuse and neglect response system are:
   1. To report suspected cases of abuse and neglect.
   2. To investigate suspected cases of abuse and neglect reported by a police call.
   3. To investigate child abuse or neglect as a by-product of other violations of the law.
   4. To provide emergency services or protection for a child in danger.

C. Law enforcement officers are sworn to uphold the law and are responsible for the welfare of the citizens they serve. They are aware of their responsibility for the publics:
   1. Safety
   2. Security
   3. Protection, even for the youngest child.

III. Various definitions of terms exist concerning the situations in which society intervenes, even against parental wishes, to protect a child's health or welfare.

A. States and communities have a variety of definitions; some are found in laws; some are found in procedures; some are found in the informal practices of the mandated agencies which implement laws concerning child abuse and neglect.

B. All professionals need to be familiar with the various formal definitions in the community such as:
   1. Those found in the Criminal Law; those forms of child abuse and neglect which are criminally punishable.
   2. Those found in the Juvenile Court Act, the Adoption Act, the Child Protective Services Act, etc. Those forms of child abuse and neglect defined in legislation which authorizes the court to require child protective services.

3. The Reporting Law definition, those forms of known or suspected child abuse, sexual abuse, and neglect which require reporting.

Method of Presentation

In this session, a group discussion of the module and its objectives will provide the learners with an overview of the material to be covered and enable them to ask questions.

The lecture method is used to present the background for police authority and the rationale behind police involvement in incidents of child abuse and neglect. A question and answer session should be used to reinforce the main points of the lecture.

Session 2: State Laws Relating to Abuse and Neglect

In Sessions 2 and 3, the Pennsylvania laws which relate to child abuse and neglect will be explored. This includes the Pennsylvania child Protective Services Act (1975), the Juvenile Act (1972), Protection from Abuse Act (1976), and the Adoption Act (1970). These Pennsylvania Acts are discussed as they pertain to the work of the police officer. The Child Protective Services Act (Act 124) and its regulations will be explored as it relates to the responsibilities involved in reporting and investigating cases of abuse and neglect. The Social Service approach to child abuse is based on Act 124. The discussion will include the who, how, what, and where of reporting and information related to the central registry, the hot-line, and confidentiality. The Protection from Abuse Act will be related to the principle of safety in one's own home. The Adoption Act will be viewed as it relates to the termination of parental rights. Legislation may vary from state to state, but the intent of protection from abuse is common to the laws in every state.

Lecture Guideslines:

I. Laws related to child abuse and neglect.
  A. The issue of police intervention in the area of child abuse and neglect is related to a number of laws statutes and acts.
    1. The criminal laws protect even the youngest child

       against acts or omissions which are considered to be detrimental to the child or the society in which the child lives.

     2. The Crime's Code specifically concerns and defines sex crimes. These apply in cases of sexual abuse of children as well as adults.

     3. The application of criminal laws to abuse and neglect justifies police intervention; however, it has not proven to be an effective deterrent.

   B. In cases where a criminal conviction is achieved.

     1. Recidivism is high.

     2. The abuser is either paroled or given a short sentence and is soon free to abuse again.

     3. The underlying causes of abuse may never be addressed.

     4. The child and his parent are placed in the adversary position of criminal and victim which discourages rehabilitation.

   C. The criminal laws and courts can be effectively used in the management and disposition of some child abuse and neglect cases.

     1. Some abusive parents' psychosis is so severe that their child's safety can only be insured by invoking the criminal court process.

     2. Some abusive parents' competency level may prevent them from coping with their children.

     3. For these parents, the most effective method of preventing abuse may be to place them in a secure, safe environment and protect their children by order of a criminal court.

   D. The criminal law may be more effective when it works in cooperation with other professionals in a treatment plan.

Discussion Questions:

1. In your opinion, should an individual accused of abuse or neglect be criminally prosecuted?

2. If your answer is yes, under what circumstances would this occur?

3. If your answer is no, what reasons would you give for this decision?
4. From your experiences, can you give examples of cases where criminal prosecution was pursued?
   — appropriately in your opinion.
   — inappropriately in your opinion.
5. What are your feelings about the appropriateness of seeking a criminal conviction in cases of abuse?
6. What are your feelings about the effectiveness of criminal conviction in cases of abuse?

Lecture Guidelines:

I. The Juvenile Act.
   A. The Juvenile Act, as related to child abuse and neglect, deals with deprived children.
      1. Deprived is defined as:
         a. Those who have been "abandoned by parents or caretakers."
         b. "Those who are without proper parental care or control."
         c. Those without proper parental "subsistence, education, or other care or control necessary for physical, mental, or emotional health, or morals."
      2. A deprived child may be taken into custody by a police or court officer if:
         a. Reasonable grounds make the officer believe that the child is suffering from illness or injury.
         b. He is in imminent danger of harm.
         c. Removal is deemed necessary for the above mentioned reasons.
      3. Under the Juvenile Act, a petition may be filed by any person if a child is deprived to determine an appropriate disposition.
      4. If a court finds a child deprived, the court may:
         a. Order the protection of the child's physical, mental or moral welfare.
         b. Permit the child to remain in his home subject to certain proscribed conditions.

    c. Remove the child from his parents and place the child in temporary custody for protection and care.

5. A deprived child may be taken into custody by a police officer if he has reasonable grounds to believe that a child is suffering from:
    a. Illness.
    b. Injury.
    c. Imminent danger of harm.

6. A child believed to be deprived and taken into custody must be brought immediately to:
    a. The court.
    b. A detention or shelter facility.
    c. A medical facility.

In all of these cases, the child's parents must be immediately notified.

7. Within 72 hours, an informal detention hearing must be held.

Method of Presentation

In this session, the lecture method will be used initially for presentation of the new material. The group discussion method will be used so that the learners may react to the presented lecture material. Copies of the applicable legislation should be provided for the learners.

In addition to being a teaching aid, this will provide the learner with a reference source in dealing with cases of abuse and neglect. After copies of the Act are handed out, the learners should break up into small groups and discuss the act in terms of their work. A recorder in each group will then present at least one question or point of discussion for the entire group's consideration. This will provide learner input and help relate the lecture to personal experiences.

The discussion should end with a review of the circumstancs under which a deprived child may be taken into custody by a police officer.

Session 3: Continuation of Laws Relating to Abuse and Neglect

This session continues the lecture and discussion of the laws that relate to abuse and neglect. Session 1 dealt with the area of general criminal law as it applied in cases of abuse and neglect. Session 2 provided an opportunity for lecture and discussion of the Juvenile Act.

Session 3 examines the Child Protective Services Law, the Protection from Abuse Act, and the Adoption act as they pertain to police work.

Content Material: Lecture Guidelines

I. Child Protective Services Law.
  A. Each of the 50 states have a reporting law.
    1. The purposes of child abuse reporting laws are:
       a. To help in the identification of abused children.
       b. To protect these children from further abuse.
       c. To provide help for the abused child and the abusive family.
    2. The Pennsylvania Reporting Law defines abused children as:
       a. A child under 18 who shows evidence of sexual abuse.
       b. A child who shows evidence of serious physical neglect.
       c. A child who shows evidence of serious physical or mental injury, of abuse not explainable as accidental by the medical history and caused by the acts or omissions of the child's parents or caretakers.
    3. If these conditions result from treatment under a bonafide religious practice, it does not constitute abuse under this act.
    4. If a child's condition is the sole result of environmental factors like inadequate housing, furnishings, income, clothing, and medical care, it should not be the basis for a finding of abuse or neglect.
    5. In most states, the Protective Services Law requires reporting of suspected child abuse and neglect by all persons who in the course of their employment, occupation, or profession come in contact with children.

6. Any person who reasonably believes that a child is abused may file a report.
7. The reporter is immune from civil and criminal liability, provided the report is made in good faith.
8. The law provides a penalty for failure to report, which makes it a legal duty for professionals to act on behalf of the children with whom they come in contact.
9. Reports of suspected child abuse or neglect are required by the Child Protective Services Law to go to the public county child welfare agency for investigation.
10. The recommended services to be provided by Child Protective Services include the following provisions:
    a. Receiving, processing, and investigating reports of suspected abuse and neglect.
    b. Maintaining a state-wide, toll-free, telephone hotline for receipt of these reports.
    c. Making a determination of abuse or risk of abuse.
    d. Initiating legal procedures.
    e. Finding temporary placement.
    f. Informing parents of the case.
    g. Counselling for children and families.
    h. Instituting educational programs.
    i. Keeping records.

Lecture Guidelines:

I. Protection from Abuse Act.
  A. This act protects family and household members from:
    1. Bodily injury.
    2. Fear of imminent bodily injury.
    3. Sexual abuse of a child by another member of the household or family.
  B. An action is started by:
    1. Filing a petition with the court.
    2. Filing a petition before a Justice of the Peace when court is not in session.
  C. If abusive behavior is proved:
    1. The court can direct the defendant to stop.

2. Evict the defendant.
3. Award to temporary custody in cases where minor children are involved.

Lecture Guidelines:

I. Adoption Act
   A. The Adoption Act concerns cases of child abuse and neglect in which the best interest of the child is not to be reunited with the natural parent. In cases where:
      1. The parents can't be located.
      2. The parents refuse to accept the child.
      3. The parents can't be responsible for the child on physical or emotional grounds.
      4. The parents have failed to provide parental care.
   B. The Adoption Act may provide for the termination of parental rights freeing the child for adoption.
   C. The grounds for involuntary termination of a parent's rights are abandonment or the failure to perform parental duties for at least six months.

Method of Presentation

In this session, the lecture method is used to present material on the Child Protective Services Law, the Protection from Abuse Act, and the Adoption Act as they pertain to the police role in child abuse and neglect situations. The Child Protective Services Law approaches the problem of child abuse from a social service point of view with the rehabilitation of the family as an important consideration. Copies of the child protective services legislation should be distributed to the group, and time should be alloted for going over the important sections presented in the lecture. The interdisciplinary approach to child abuse will be further explored in later sesions.

Following the lectures, copies of the Protection From Abuse Act and the Adoption Act should be provided for the group. After examining the handouts, the groups should be given time to ask questions concerning the laws in their particular state.

The case study technique is used as a method for clarifying, summarizing, and reinforcing the presented material. The case study approach will relate the information in the lectures to simulated work situations. The case is presented in two parts; each part has a set of related discussion questions.

The material included for this session involves a variety of teaching methods. The trainer should select the methods with which he or she feels most confident.

Resource Material:

Discussion Case: Part 1

In answer to a call from a neighbor regarding a case of child neglect, Officers Andrews and Hartman proceeded to Apartment 14 at 343 Wilder Place to investigate the complaint. Upon arrival at the scene, the officers found the apartment secured by an old and tattered screen door. The door was locked, but the holes in the screening were large enough to reach in and unhook the door. Looking in through the screen door, the officers could see a very dirty small apartment. The floor was covered with garbage spilled from several upset garbage bags and glass from broken bottles. The officers noticed a toddler about two years old playing among the broken bottles and empty tin cans. The child was bleeding from a cut on the right thigh and was crying. After the officers knocked several times and called for Mrs. Paladino, she came to the door. Mrs. Paladino appeared to be under the influence of alcohol or other substance. The officers told Mrs. Paladino that they were investigating a complaint that her children were in danger, but she seemed unable to understand and wandered away when the officers asked if they could enter the apartment.

Discussion Questions for Part I:

1. Do the officers have the legal right to enter the apartment?
2. If you answer yes, why?
3. If you answer no, why?
4. Discuss the possible alternative actions that the police officers could take.

Discussion Case Part 2:

The officers reached in and unlocked the screen door and entered the apartment because they believed that Mrs. Paladino's condition and the appearance of the home placed the children in imminent danger. In addition to the filth the officers first observed, they discovered that the toilet was clogged and had overflowed onto the bathroom floor. The refrigerator was almost empty, except for a few cans of beer and some moldy hot dogs.

In the crib was a small six-month-old baby who appeared quite fragile. The toddler he had first seen appeared in good health except for the bleeding thigh cut. Mrs. Paladino was becoming belligerent toward the officers. The officers questioned her about her eldest child, a 6-year-old son. Upon questioning, Mrs. Paladino revealed that her son, Ricco, had gone to the store several hours ago and had not yet returned.

Discussion Questions for Part 2:

1. Is there probable cause for placing the children in protective custody? Why or why not?
2. If so, how would this be accomplished?
3. If not, what should the officers do at this time?
4. What actions should be taken regarding the missing 6 year old?
5. What, if any other, agencies should be contacted?

Session 4: Legal Case Flow

The legal proceedings which follow a report of abuse and/or neglect will be traced in this session. Reference will be made to the laws of abuse and neglect examined in the previous sessions, as they relate to the legal proceedings to be outlined in this session. Some terms will be defined as they apply to the legal process in cases of abuse and neglect.

Any discipline's involvement in cases of abuse and neglect may be intermittent. An overview of the entire system from report to final adjudication will enable them to see the relevance of their role in a complex and interdisciplinary community problem. This session will correlate the information previously presented with this and future sessions. Tracing the legal flow of a case includes the way in which a variety of professionals must share the responsibility for the protection of children.

Content Material:

I. Definition of terms.
  A. The following interdisciplinary definitions are related to the understanding of child abuse and neglect situations.
    1. An *adjudication hearing* is a court hearing in which it is decided whether or not charges against a parent or caretaker are substantiated by admissible evidence. This hearing is also known as a jurisdictional or evidentiary hearing.
    2. *Admissible evidence* is evidence which may be legally and properly used in court.
    3. An *affidavit* is a written statement signed in the presence of a notary public who "swears in" the signer. The contents of the affidavit are stated under penalty of perjury. Affidavits are frequently used in the initiation of juvenile court cases and are, at times, presented to the court as evidence.
    4. An *allegation* is a charge or complaint which is proven true or false at a hearing or trial. In a child abuse or neglect case, the allegation is a petition or statement containing charges of specific acts of cruelty or improper care which the petitioner hopes to prove at a trial.
    5. An *appeal* is a resort to a higher court in the attempt to have a decision of a trial court changed. Usually, appeals are made and decided upon questions of law only. Issues of fact (eg., Did the minor suffer an accident, or was he intentionally injured?) are left to the trial judge or jury and seldom can be redecided in an appeal.
    6. The *interest of the child* is a standard for deciding among

alternative plans for abused or neglected children. Here, the least detrimental alternative principle governs. Usually it is in the child's best interest and least detrimental if the child remains in the home, provided that the parents can respond to treatment. However, this decision may be difficult until it is known whether the necessary resources are available. A few authorities believe that except where the child's life is in danger, it is always in the child's best interest to remain in the home. In evaluating the least determinal alternative and the child's best interest, the child's psychological as well as physical well-being must be considered. In developing a plan, the best interest of the child may carry less weight than parental rights or agency policy and practice. However, if the least detrimental alternative principle is utilized, the child's best interest will be served. The best interest of the child and least detrimental alternative principles resulted as a reaction to the overuse of child placement in cases of abuse and neglect. "The best interest of the child" suggests that some placement may be justified, but "least detrimental alternative" is stronger in suggesting that any placement or alternative should be monitored.

7. The *burden of proof* is the duty, usually falling on the state as petitioner, of proving allegations against a parent in a trial. The state must prove the case; neither the child nor the parents must respond to unproven allegations.

8. *A child is a person*, also known as a minor, from birth to legal age of maturity for whom a parent and/or caretaker, foster parent, public or private home, institution, or agency is legally responsible. Some child abuse legislation defines a child as a person under eighteen. In some states, a person of any age with a developmental disability is defined as a child.

9. *Children's rights* are rights of children as individuals to the protections provided in the Constitution as well as

to the care and protection necessary for normal growth and development. Children's rights are actually exercised through adult representatives and advocates. The extent to which children's rights are protected varies according to the individual state laws providing for the identification and treatment of child abuse and neglect. An unresolved issue is in the conflict between children's rights and parent's rights or rights to privacy.

10. A *civil proceeding* is any lawsuit other than criminal prosecutions. Juvenile and family court cases are civil proceedings or civil actions.

11. A *complaint* is: 1. An oral statement, usually made to the police, charging criminal, abusive, or neglectful conduct.
    2. A district attorney's document which starts a criminal prosecution.
    3. A petitioner's document which starts a civil proceeding. In juvenile or family court, the complaint is usually called a petition.
    4. In some state, term used for a report of suspected abuse or neglect.

12. *Confidentiality* is the professional practice of not sharing with others information entrusted by a client or patient. Sometimes communications between parent and physician or social worker are expected to be confidential but are later used in court, and many physicians and social workers are torn between legal and professional obligations. Confidentiality, which is protected by statute, is known as priviledged communications. Confidentiality need not obstruct information sharing if a multidisciplinary team has established policy and guidelines on confidentiality.

13. *The courts* are places where judicial proceedings occur. An array of courts are involved with child abuse and neglect cases, partly because different states divide responsibility for certain proceedings among different courts, and also because tradition has established a va-

riety of names for courts which perform similar functions. Child abuse reports can result in proceedings in any of the following courts:

a. Domestic Relations Court is a civil court in which divorces and divorce custody hearings are held.

b. Family Court is a civil court which, in some states, combines the functions of domestic relations, juvenile, and probate courts. Establishment of family courts is often urged to reform the presently wasteful and poorly - coordinated civil court system. Under some proposals, family courts would also deal with criminal cases involving family relations, thus improving coordination in child abuse litigation.

c. The Juvenile Court is a court which has jurisdiction over minors and usually handles cases of suspected delinquency as well as cases of suspected abuse or neglect. In many states, termination of parental rights occurs in juvenile court proceedings, but that is generally the limit of juvenile court's power over adults.

d. The Probate Court is a court which may handle cases of guardianship and adoption in addition to estates of deceased persons.

14. *Custody* is the right to care and control a child and the duty to provide food, clothing, shelter, ordinary medical care, education, and discipline. Permanent legal custody may be taken from a parent or given up by a parent by court action. Temporary custody may be granted for a period of months or, in the case of protective or emergency custody, for a period of hours or several days.

a. Emergency custody involves the ability of a law enforcement officer, pursuant to the criminal code, to take temporary custody of a child who is in immediate danger and place him or her in the control of Child Protective Services. A custody hearing must usually be held within 72 hours of such action. Emergency custody is also known as police custody.

    b. Protective custody is the emergency measure taken to detain a child, often in a hospital, until a written detention request can be filed. In some states, telephone communication with a judge is required to authorize protective custody. In other states, police, social workers, or doctors have statutory authority to detain minors who are in imminent danger.

15. A *custory hearing* is a hearing held in family division or juvenile division to determine who has the rights of legal custody of a minor. It may involve one parent against the other or the parents versus a social service agency.

16. *Dependency* is a child's need for care and supervision from a parent or caretaker. Often this legal term refers to cases in which natural parent(s) cannot or will not properly care for children or supervise them, so the state must assume this responsibility. Many states distinguish findings of dependency, for which the juvenile has little or no responsibility, from findings of delinquency in which the juvenile is at least partially responsible for his or her behavior.

17. *Detention* is the temporary confinement of a person by a public authority. In a case of child abuse or neglect, a child may be detained pending a trial when a detention hearing indicates that the child is unsafe in his or her own home. Such detention is often called protective custody or emergency custody. The child may be detained in a foster home, group home, hospital, or other facility.

18. A *disposition* is the order of a juvenile or family court issued at a dispositional hearing which determines whether a minor already found dependent or delinquent should remain in or return to the parental home, and under what kind of supervision, or whether the minor should be placed out of the home, in a relative's home, a foster home, or an institution. Disposition in a civil case parallels sentencing in a criminal case.

19. *Due process* is the right of persons involved in legal pro-

ceedings to be treated with fairness. These rights include the right to adequate notice in advance of hearings, the right to notice of allegations of misconduct, the right to the assistance of a lawyer, the right to confront and cross-examine witnesses, and the right to refuse to give self-incriminating testimony. In child abuse or neglect cases, courts are granting more and more due process to parents, because loss of parental rights, temporarily or permanently, is as serious as loss of liberty. However, jury trials and presumptions of innocence are still afforded in very few juvenile or family court cases.

20. *Evidence* is any sort of proof submitted to the court for the purpose of influencing the court's decision:

a. Circumstantial evidence is proof of circumstances which may imply another fact. For example, proof that a parent kept a broken appliance cord may indicate that the parent infliced marks on a child's body.

b. Direct evidence consists of testimony, such as a neighbor saying he or she saw the parent strike the child with an appliance cord.

c. Hearsay evidence is second-hand evidence, testimony such as "I heard him say . . . ." Except in certain cases, such evidence is excluded because it is considered unreliable and because the person making the original statement cannot be cross-examined.

d. Opinion is evidence given by an expert. Although witnesses are ordinarily not permitted to testify to their beliefs or opinions, being restricted to what they actually saw or heard, a witness can be qualified as an expert on a given subject. Then he or she can report his or her conclusions, for example, "Based upon these marks, it is my opinion as a doctor that the child must have been struck with a flexible instrument very much like this appliance cord." Lawyers are sometimes allowed to ask qualified experts "hypothetical questions," in which the witness is given certain facts and asked to express an opinion based on those "facts."

e. Physical evidence is any tangible piece of proof such as a document, x-ray, photograph, or weapon used to inflict an injury. Physical evidence must usually be authenticated by a witness who testifies to the connection of the evidence (also called an exhibit) with other facts in the case.

21. *Evidentiary Standards* are guidelines used when examining evidence in order to determine if that evidence is factual and legally proves the case being tried. Various standards of proof are.

a. Beyond a Reasonable Doubt (criminal court standard). The evidence presented fully satisfies the court as being factual.

b. Clear and Convincing Evidence (standard in many abuse/neglect cases). The evidence is fully convincing and equivalent to beyond a reasonable doubt.

c. Preponderance of Evidence (civil court standard). The evidence leaves the court with the strongest impression of credibility and is determined to be fact.

22. *Exhibit* is the physical evidence used in court. In a child abuse case, an exhibit may consist of x-rays, photographs of the child's injuries, or the actual materials presumably used to inflict the injuries.

23. *Expert testimony* is given by witnesses with various types of expertise who testify in child abuse or neglect cases; usually these expert witnesses are physicians or radiologists. Experts are usually questioned in court about their education or experience which qualify them to give professional opinions about the matter in question. Only after the hearing officer determines the expertise of the witness in the subject matter may that witness state his or her opinions.

24. A *founded report* is any report of suspected child abuse or neglect made to the mandated agency which is con-

firmed or verified by the court. Founded reports outnumber unfounded reports.

25. A *guardian* is an adult charged lawfully with the responsibility for a child. A guardian has almost all the rights and powers of a natural parent, but the relationship is subject to termination or change. A guardian may or may not also have custody, the actual care and supervision of the child.

26. A *guardian ad litem* (GAL) is an adult appointed by the court to represent the child in a judicial proceeding. The guadian ad litem may be, but is not necessarily, an attorney (state laws vary). Under the Child Abuse Prevention and Treatment Act, a state cannot qualify for federal assistance unless it provides by statute "that in every case involving an abused or neglected child which results in a judicial proceeding a guardian ad litem shall be appointed to represent the child in such proceedings." Some states have begun to allow a GAL for children in divorce cases.

27. A *hearing* is a judicial proceeding in which issues of fact or law are tried and in which both parties have a right to be heard. A hearing is synonymous with a trial.

28. An *in camera hearing* is a closed hearing before a judge in his chambers.

29. *Jurisdiction* is the power of a particular court to hear cases involving certain categories of persons or allegations. Jurisdiction may also depend upon geographical factors such as the county of a person's residence.

30. *Parents Patriae* means "The power of the sovereign" and refers to the state's power to act for or on behalf of persons who are unable: minors, incompetents, or some developmentally disabled.

31. A *petition* is a document filed in juvenile court or family court at the beginning of a neglect, abuse, and/or delinquency case. The petition states the allegations which, if true, form the basis for court intervention.

32. A *petitioner* is a person who files a petition. In juvenile court practice, anyone may be a petitioner.

33. *Privileged communications* are confidential communications which are protected by statutes and need not or cannot be disclosed in court over the objections of the holder of the privilege. Lawyers almost always may refuse to disclose what a client has told them in confidence. Priests are similarly covered. Doctors and psychotherapists have generally lesser privileges, and their testimony can be compelled in many cases involving child abuse or neglect. Some social workers are covered by such statutes, but the law and practice vary widely from state to state.

34. *Reviews of dependency cases* are periodic reviews to determine whether continued child placement or court supervision of a child are necessary. Increasingly required by state law, such reviews by the court also provide some judicial supervision of probation or case work services.

35. *Termination of parental rights* (TPR) is a legal proceeding freeing a child from his or her parents' claims so that the child may be adopted by others without the parents' written consent. The legal bases for termination differ from state to state, but most statutes include abandonment as grounds for TPR.

Lecture Guidelines:

I. Legal case flow.
   A. A simulated case situation sets the legal process in motion.
      1. A case of suspected abuse is reported to the police.
      2. The police officer notifies Children and Youth Services that he is taking the battered child to Children's Hospital.
      3. Most reports from hospitals consist of requests for restraining orders.
         a. Issued by the judges, the orders prevent parents from removing their child from the hospital.
         b. The Juvenile Act requires a hearing within 72 hours after the issuing of the order.
      4. The filing of a petition without a shelter hearing is relatively rare.

a. Most court cases involve children who are unable or unwilling to live at home.
b. The only cases in which a petition would be filed without a shelter hearing are the occasional truancy cases.
c. Most truancy comes to the attention of the court in conjunction with more severe in-home problems.
5. The Juvenile Act requires a petition within 24 hours of admission.
6. Specific time requirements may vary according to the laws in a particular state.
   a. Children and Youth Services may interpret this rule as not including weekends and holidays.
7. At the shelter hearing, the child advocate attorney will first meet the child (if she or he is old enough or well enough to be brought to court) to find out the basic details of the case.
8. The act requires a hearing within 10 days if the child is placed at a shelter.
9. If, at the shelter hearing, the case may be one which can be solved easily without extensive court involvement.
   a. The parent may need to find housing.
   b. The child may be from out of state.
   c. Judges will continue the shelter hearing for a few weeks until the problem is resolved and the children are returned home.
   d. At that point, court activity would be discontinued without a formal hearing.
10. The Juvenile Act divides the full hearing:
   a. The stages are the adjudicatory phase and the disposition phase.
   b. Some states do hold two separate hearings.
11. At the full hearing, the Judge may dismiss the petition, making a finding of dependency:
   a. He may continue the hearing without a formal finding.
   b. If he dismisses the petition, court involvement ends.

      c. Most judges will continue the hearing without a formal finding if the child has a chance to be returned home.

      d. Even with a finding of dependency, most judges will hold continued hearings or review hearings, at least until the child is placed.

12. Because legislation and accompanying case laws mandate that children be with their natural parents whenever possible, judges will usually try to return younger children to their homes.

13. Some judges will go to extraordinary lengths to place a child with relatives.

      a. Less frequently, they will place the child with friends.

      b. Some judges firmly believe that a child should be kept within the extended family and should be kept out of the judicial system.

      c. If a relative, or for older children, a neighbor comes to the shelter hearing or first full hearing, some judges may place the child with them.

14. If the court decides that a child needs to be placed away from home, and an appropriate placement is available, the child will be placed immediately.

15. Often, however, no immediate openings exist, and the child has to remain at shelter for a few weeks to six months.

      a. Most judges will continue to hold review hearings to ensure that the child is properly placed.

Case Flow Chart:

  I. Introduction to Case Flow Chart.

    A. The primary goal of traditional police investigations is the discovery of evidence to prove that a crime has been committed and that a specific person committed the crime. Neglect and abuse investigations differ from traditional police cases in that their goal is the protection of the child rather than the prosecution of the abuser.

II. Discussion Questions:

1. How do you determine whether abuse or neglect has occured?
   a. Is the child safe in its present environment?
   b. Is the child safe with its parents or caretakers?
   c. Does the child need protective custody?
2. Should the child be referred to Children and Youth Services?
3. Should the child be referred to some other community agency?
   a. Is hospital care required?
   b. Should someone be arrested?

Method of Presentation

The session will begin with a brief review of the laws which govern law enforcement involvement in child abuse and neglect cases. Next a lecture and a class discussion of the relevant terms used in cases of abuse. The trainer must decide on the amount of time allotted to each definition based on the knowledge displayed by the learners during the group discussion.

The role-playing profile from Module V, Session 3, describes a child who appears to have a broken leg and other visible bruises. This role-playing profile will provide the initial step into the legal process. The legal case flow will be examined and discussed. The case flow will be presented in chronological sequence, stopping at proscribed intervals to allow learner input. Some of the learners will have had experiences with parts of the legal process. The discussion which precedes the lecture will help determine the emphasis to be placed on the various steps in the legal process. A flow chart will be used to enable the learners to visualize the presentation.

Copies of the provided case flow chart should be distributed to the class. The main points of the lecture and discussion will be reviewed and related to the points on the flow chart.

Discussion questions have been provided along with the case flow chart. The questions should lead to discussion of the ineffectiveness of criminal prosecution in cases of abuse and neglect and should introduce the social service and multidisciplinary approaches to abuse which will be discussed further in the following module.

Resources: Required for the Instructor as Background for Teaching Module V

1. Flammang, C.J., *The Police and the Underprotected Child.* Springfield, Illinois: Charles C Thomas, 1970.

This text is written from the law enforcement point of view. It correlates the role of police personnel with the task of protection of children.

2. Helfer, R.E., and Kempe, C.H., *The Battered Child, 2nd Edition.* Chicago: University of Chicago Press, 1980.

The contributors of this book concern themselves with such issues as history, incidence, reporting, intervention and treatment of cases of abuse. The role and responsibility of law enforcement is included.

3. U.S. Dept. of Health and Human Services, *Interdisciplinary Glossary on Child Abuse and Neglect.* Administration for Children, Youth, and Families, Children's Bureau. National Center on Child Abuse and Neglect, 1980.

This glossary of terms presents definitions accepted by a variety of disciplines, and all professionals should have a working knowledge of the common language of abuse.

4. Juvenile Act 11 P.S. 50-101, Dec. 6, 1972. P.L. 1464, No. 333
5. Child Protective Services Law, 11 P.S. 2201, Nov. 26, 1975
6. Adoption Act, 1 P.S. 101, July 24, 1970. P.L. 620, No. 208
7. Protection From Abuse Act, 35 P.S. 10181, Oct. 7, 1976. P.L. No. 218

All of the abuse and neglect laws relevant to the particular state in which the training is conducted.

CASE FLOW CHART

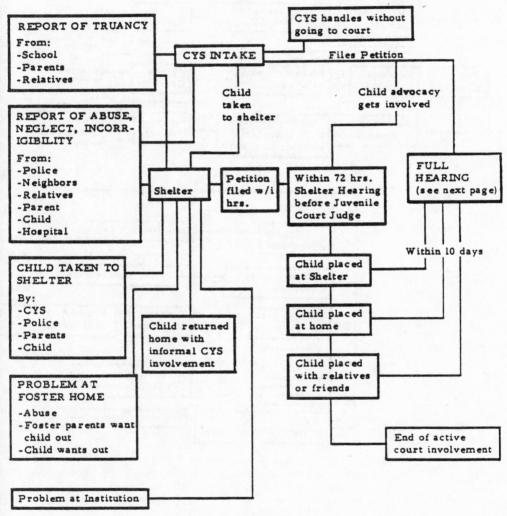

Figure 1

CASE FLOW CHART (con't)

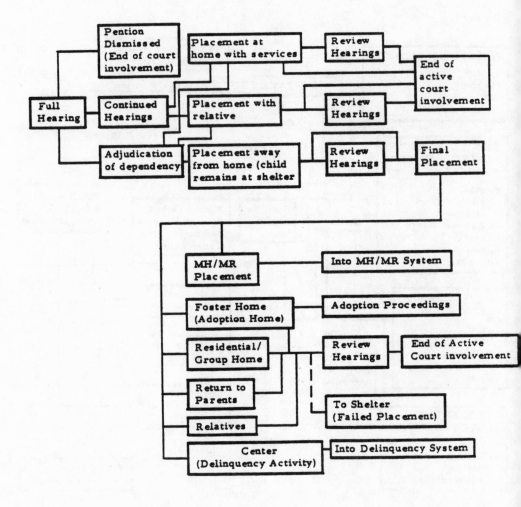

CHAPTER 6

MODULE VI — THE COMMUNITY RESOURCES THAT DEAL WITH CHILD ABUSE AND NEGLECT

MODULE OVERVIEW

THIS module presents a description of the resources in the community that deal with child abuse and neglect: Children and Youth Services, Community Agencies, Juvenile and Criminal Court and Social Service Agencies. The responsibilities and services of each of these agencies are explored.

Objectives

1. To maintain professional standards in dealing with cases of physical and sexual abuse.
2. To utilize relevant knowledge about laws and available social agencies in cases of child abuse and neglect.
3. To increase awareness of the community resources that deal with child abuse and neglect.
4. To increase awareness of the contributions made by the various disciplines in cases of child abuse and neglect.
5. To acquaint trainees with the roles of the various disciplines involved in the reporting and referral process.

Schedule:

Session 1: Community Resources
Session 2: Professionals Involved from Referral to Treatment
Session 3: Hospital Procedure

Session 1: Community Resources

This module focuses on the community resources and the disciplines within those agencies that participate in the multifaceted problem of child abuse and neglect. A knowledge and understanding of the community systems and their respective functions will better prepare all professionals to collaborate within the resource network for the protection of children.

Content Material: Discuss Module Objectives.

Introductory Discussion Questions:

1. What are the community systems involved in cases of abuse and neglect (See Figure 1)?
2. Why are there continuous lines between all of these systems on the community resource chart (See Figure 1)?
3. In what way might Children and Youth Services utilize some of the other systems in the network:
4. In what way might the health professions utilize some of the other systems?
5. In what way might private and/or public treatment facilities utilize some of the other systems?
6. In what way might schools utilize the other systems?
7. In what way might the courts be involved with other systems?
8. In what way might the police become involved with the other systems in the network?

Lecture Guidelines:

    I. Community systems.
       A. Children and Youth Services.
          1. Children and youth Services in the agency with the primary responsibility for child abuse and neglect, prevention, and treatment.
          2. This agency reaches out with a variety of social services to strengthen the family unit.
          3. These services may mean referral to the other system including:
            a. Medical.

      b. Psychological.

      c. Courts.

      d. Police.

   4. Children and Youth Services is responsible for the family situation until the conditions are treated and neglect is reduced.

B. Community agencies.

   1. A number of treatment facilities, both public and private, can offer help for the family in crisis.

   2. Group homes offer shelter for adolescents, give family counselling to both the abusive parents and foster parents:

      a. The family treatment centers offer shelter and counselling.

      b. Parents United is a program of treatment and counselling for victims of sexual abuse.

      c. Parents Anonymous is a nationwide self-help organization for the prevention and treatment of child abuse.

   3. Each community has a variety of agencies that can become involved with cases of neglect and/or abuse in a number of different ways.

C. Medical facilities.

   1. Many hospitals are sensitive to the problem of abuse and neglect. They have social workers on their staff who are prepared to investigate and report suspected cases of abuse.

   2. Many large city hospitals have been active in aiding research in child abuse and neglect.

   3. Many hospitals have policies and procedures for managing and reporting suspected cases of abuse.

   4. Physicians in private practice seem to be more cautious about involvement in the reporting process, especially in higher socioeconomic areas.

D. School systems.

   1. In the classroom, abuse cases may be recognized early if teachers are aware of the problem and the school administration has policies and procedures to insure the

reporting of suspected abuse.

2. For an abused child, day care centers and public school classrooms may provide the first out-of-home contact where help is available.

E. Court system.

1. The Juvenile Courts have a unique coercive but non-punitive authority to assist Children and Youth Services in getting parents into a treatment plan.

2. Court action can bring attention to the extent of the problem, review its causes, and recommend solutions.

Discussion Guidelines:

I. Community resources.

A. Effective as well as ineffective professionals exist in every discipline.

1. What have been your experiences with professionals from community resources?

2. In your opinion, were they effective?

3. If so, how? If not, why?

B. A discussion of the learner's personal experiences with community resource personnel will help to:

1. Clarify misconceptions about other disciplines.

2. Explore feelings and attitudes related to other disciplines and their handling of abuse cases.

3. Reveal feelings and attitudes about physical and sexual abuse cases so that they may be examined and discussed.

4. Make the material of this session more meaningful by relating it to personal experiences.

5. Examine old prejudices and preconceived ideas of other professionals.

6. Broaden the learner's view of the complexities of child abuse and neglect.

Method of Presentation

An overview of the module contents and objectives will be presented in the first session. The community resources available for the enormous task of protecting children from abuse and neglect will be discussed. The lecture method will be used for the presentation of new materials. Group discussion, using Figure 2, will help to determine learner input levels as well as serve as a feedback mechanism for the trainer.

The community resource systems should be listed on the chalkboard (Figure 2). The interdependence of community systems should be explored by means of the introductory discussion questions provided. These questions are used to introduce the material in the lecture and to encourage discussion regarding the community resources available for protecting abused children and their families.

The summary discussion guidelines provide an opportunity for the trainer to summarize the important points in the lecture while encouraging class discussion of the practical application of the presented material.

Resource Material: Chalkboard Diagram — Community Resource Chart — Figure 2.

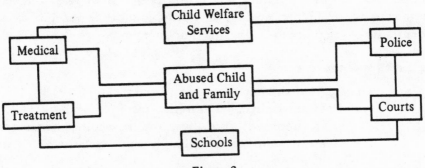

Figure 2

Session 2: Professionals Involved from Referral to Treatment

A brief review of the various community resources presented in Session 1 will introduce the topic of Session 2. The environmental forces that influence the community systems involved in abuse and neglect (media, economy, etc.) will be explored. Within each of the systems mentioned is a variety of professionals. Each discipline makes a valuable contribution to the family in crisis. All professionals must have knowledge and awareness of the contributions made by these various disciplines. This session explores the contributions of professionals from report to treatment in cases of abuse and/or neglect.

Since Sessions 2 and 3 deal with the involvement of a variety of professionals in cases of abuse and neglect, the trainer should call upon the services of several professionals in the community for a panel discussion approach to this material. This approach provides much needed interaction between disciplines. Professionals must have a clear understanding of the contributions of the various disciplines in order to have a complete picture of the process involved in helping abusive families. A panel made up of a hospital social worker, a psychologist, and a representative from Children and Youth Services would have greater impact on the topic of this session, the involvement of professionals in cases of abuse from referral to treatment. This panel would also introduce these community professionals to the learners so that in future situations they may feel better about making referrals to these agencies. A presentation format followed by a question and answer period is advised. The following material is provided for the trainer and/or the panel to use as a frame of reference to be expanded or augmented.

Lecture Guidelines:

    I. Referral to treatment.
       A. Professionals involved in initial stages.
          1. The initial report of abuse and neglect may be phoned directly into the Childline Telephone System or hotline.
          2. Each toll-free line is answered directly by a telephone counselor.
          3. The childline worker processes the report and enters it in the pending complaint file.
          4. The complaint is held in the pending complaint file which contains the reports of suspected abuse under investigation by Child Protective Service Units.
          5. Those reports of child abuse which were determined to be founded or indicated are contained in the Central Register Section.

     a. Founded means that an adjudication has been based on a finding that said has been abused.

     b. Indicated means that substantial evidence of the alleged abuse exists.

6. The childline worker secures as much information as possible from the caller.

7. The Central Register is checked for prior reports.

     a. A case number is assigned.

     b. The Child Protective Services Unit is immediately and completely informed, both orally and in writing.

8. Reports received directly by Child Protective Services units are relayed to the childline and are handled in the same way.

9. Within hours of receipt of a report of suspected abuse, many people have been involved.

     a. A telephone counselor must be able to get complete and accurate information from what may be a reluctant, troubled, excited, or frightened caller.

     b. The information must be processed.

     c. The appropriate Child Protective Service must be completely informed, both orally and in writing.

10. On a daily basis, the childline staff monitors the reports in the pending complaint file to determine if the follow-up reports are received within the 30-and 60-day time periods proscribed by law in most states.

11. All reports received by childline are confidential by law and may be made available only to proscribed recipients.

     a. This includes "any person, agency or institutions upon written consent of all subjects of the report."

     b. Child Protective Services as the primary agent is aided by a variety of professionals.

B. Teamwork aids in the protection of the child and reduces friction between agencies.

  1. Child Protective Services offered to the abused child and his family are.

     a. To investigate reports.

     b. To take the child into protective custody.

     c. To provide rehabilitation services to the family.

2. This requires the input and cooperation of a number of professionals in various disciplines:

     a. Investigators.

     b. Shelter personnel.

     c. Counselors.

     d. Psychologists.

     e. Medical personnel.

     f. Legal personnel.

     g. Law enforcement personnel.

     h. Judges.

     i. A coroner.

3. No one system or agency can handle this complex problem without the aid of related disciplines.

C. Many professionals are involved in a case of abuse or neglect.

1. The report of suspected abuse may come from a variety of sources: the police, a doctor, a teacher, a nurse, etc.

2. The report goes to Child Protective Services.

3. A social worker investigates the report, perhaps with the aid of the police depending on the circumstances of the case.

4. If intervention is needed, a doctor, psychologists, phychiatrist, social worker, visiting nurse, etc. will work with the child and his family.

5. In some cases, court intervention may be needed to get protective custody of the child.

6. The Gault case brought legal representation to minors as a constitutional right. Because of this court decision, child advocacy attorneys are involved in cases of abuse.

7. Court involvement may require law enforcement, lawyers, judges, and community placement facilities.

8. Clearly, many professionals are involved in cases of abuse, and they must cooperate with other professionals and nonprofessionals.

9. From the initial report of suspected abuse to the disposition and final treatment plan, the cooperation and
coordination of professionals is necessary.

Discussion Guidelines:

1. Is it necessary for so many diciplines to become involved in cases
of abuse?
2. If so, why? If not, why?
3. With which disciplines have you had good working experience?
4. With which disciplines have you had bad working experiences?
5. What might have been done to improve the working relationship?
6. How do you feel about the abusive parent's right to privacy and
confidentiality?

Method of Presentation

The lecture material will present the way in which a case pro-
gresses through the many resource systems involved. Leader-
centered and group discussion sessions will serve as a feedback
mechanism. Discussions will relate the learner's own experiences to
the lecture material and will clarify some of the learner's feelings and
attitudes toward human service agencies.

Discussion questions have been provided as a follow-up to the
lecture and discussion techniques. At this time, the trainer should
emphasize the points in the lecture concerning the Children and
Youth Services as the agency primarily responsible for child abuse
and neglect prevention and treatment. Because of the complexity of
the problem, it is best handled by a coordination of Child Protective
Services staff, specially-trained law enforcement personnel, and a
variety of professionals.

Session 3: Hospital Procedure

Children and Youth Services is only one of many community resources that may call upon police services in cases of abuse and
neglect. In this session, the interaction of hospital and medical professionals with the police, when abuse is suspected, will be explored.
Some procedures that require police involvement in hospital policy
will be discussed. If the suggested format of a panel of professionals

is used, then the material in Sessions 2 and 3 will be combined and presented together. The following materials may be used as a frame of reference for the trainer to use alone or in combination with other professionals.

Content Material: Lecture Guidelines

I. Urban Hospital procedures.
   A. The police officer should know what is being done for the child he brings to a hospital, when abuse is suspected.
      1. Many cases of suspected abuse are confirmed when children are brought to a hospital emergency room.
      2. All children under the age of two entering the hospital are, by policy and procedure, admitted if abuse is suspected. These children are also given a skeletal survey.
      3. Because children under two are most vulnerable, admission is always recommended.
      4. These admissions are then immediately reported to the Social Work Department of the hospital.
      5. When abuse is suspected in children over the age of two, the physician should contact the emergency room social worker before a decision is made regarding case management.
      6. If a hospital work-up is done, it will include:
         a. A complete physical.
         b. A skeletal survey.
         c. Color photographs.
         d. Laboratory studies.
         e. Assessment of psychomotor development.
         f. Nursing notes on parent-child interaction.
      7. In cases where the decision is not to admit, the child may be sent to a Children and Youth Services Reception Center.
      8. In emergency situations, police assistance is requested to transport the child.
      9. In cases of sexual abuse and rape, most hospitals have developed a set of procedures in consultation with:
         a. An Interagency Task Force on Rape Related Services.

    b. A local rape center.

    c. The Center for Victims of Violent Crime.

    d. Law Enforcement Agencies.

  10. These procedures tend to leave the decision to report the incident to the discretion of the family.

  11. The two basic elements in managing sexual assault victims are:

    a. Care of the patient.

    b. Participation in the criminal investigatory system.

  12. The role of medical personnel in this area is:

    a. Verification of the assault.

    b. Identification of the assailant.

  13. The physician has a responsibility to:

    a. Perform the evaluation.

    b. Provide the treatment.

    c. Collect the appropriate specimens.

    d. Fill out the required records relative to the investigation.

  14. In many instances of rape, the incident has been reported to the police before the hospital visit.

  15. If police have not been notified, they must be if the victim was physically injured during the sexual assault.

  16. In the absence of physical injury, the assault should still be reported unless the mentally-competent victim requests that it not be reported.

  17. Reporting does not mean that prosecution must be pursued; however, it makes prosecution easier if decided on later.

  18. Reporting also alerts the police of the potential danger to other citizens.

  19. If a family member is the suspected assailant, most states require that the police be notified.

II. General hospital policy regarding abuse.

 A. The Social Service Department may report interaction with the police in the following areas:

  1. When a police officer brings a child to the emergency room and states that abuse and/or neglect is suspected.

  2. In cases where transportation to a shelter becomes necessary.

3. In cases where the parents take the child from the hospital before the child has been released. The police are given a restraining order which enables them to take the child from the home and return him to the hospital.

The film, *Barb: Breaking the Cycle of Child Abuse*, is recommended for use at this time. The film deals with the community resources available for helping in cases of abuse. This 28-minute color film is available through the Department of Public Welfare, Welfare Press and Publications Office, Audio Visual Section, Harrisburg, Pennsylvania.

Method of Presentation

The recommended method of presentation for Sessions 2 and 3 is a panel discussion format by a group of professionals. Lecture guidelines have been provided for the presentation of new material if the trainer is conducting the sessions alone or with these other professionals.

A brief review of the community systems and the ways in which they interact with the police in abuse and neglect cases will correlate the lecture material of all three module sessions. The review will also provide a lead-in to the film, *Barb: Breaking the Cycle of Child Abuse*, which deals with some of the community resources available to help in cases of abuse. The film will deal with solutions and alternatives to the problem of abuse. Every community has the resources that were discussed in previous sessions. This film shows how these resources can work for the benefit of the abusive family. The film will bring together and review the content presented in the previous sessions of the module. Some comments regarding the film should be made before viewing, and a discussion period should follow the film. The trainer should obtain and review this film well in advance of its use as a teaching aid in Module VI, Session 3. A discussion resulting from the viewing of the film should follow.

Resources: Required for the Instructor as Background for Teaching Module VI

1. Bard, M., The Role of Law Enforcement in the Helping System,

Community Mental Health Journal, 1971.

This article provides background and current information concerning law enforcement's role as a partner in the community-wide resource system of aid for abusive families.

2. Bard, M., *The Function of Police in Crisis Intervention and Conflict Management*. U.S. Department of Justice, L.E.A.A. Washington, D.C.: Criminal Justice Associates, Inc., 1975.

This publication outlines the function of law enforcement in cooperation with health care professionals in family crisis intervention.

3. DeFrancis, V., *Protecting the Abused Child — A Coordinated Approach*. A National Symposium on Child Abuse. Denver: The American Humane Association.

This publication's approach to the topic of protection of the abused child concerns the cooperation and coordination of the disciplines invovled.

4. Garbarino, J., and Gillian, G., *Understanding Abusive Families*. Lexington, Mass.: Heath Co., 1980.

This text deals with background information and new knowledge with sensitivity and understanding in the handling of abusive families.

5. Film — *Barb: Breaking the Cycle of Child Abuse.*

A color film, 1978, 28 minutes. Available through the Department of Public Welfare, Welfare Press and Publications Office, Audio Visual Section, Harrisburg, Pennsylvania.

CHAPTER 7

MODULE VII — THE PROFESSIONAL'S ROLE ON MULTIDISCIPLINARY TEAMS DEALING WITH CHILD ABUSE AND NEGLECT

MODULE OVERVIEW

THIS module presents the working relationship between law enforcement, social services, and health care professionals in investigating suspected cases of child abuse and neglect. Child abuse is discussed as a community problem which requires cooperative efforts with Children and Youth Services, hospitals, law enforcement personnel, and the judicial system. The importance of interagency cooperation is emphasized.

Objectives

1. To improve knowledge and skills of the many professionals involved in cases of child abuse and neglect.
2. To improve the cooperation between these professionals and the social agencies that investigate cases of child abuse and neglect.
3. To clarify the function of the law enforcement in cases of child abuse and neglect.
4. To foster cooperative efforts among law enforcement, Children and Youth Services, Children's Hospital, and other community agencies in dealing with the problem of abuse.
5. To enhance the role of all professionals as advocates for the prevention of child abuse and neglect.

Schedule:

Session 1: Child Abuse and Neglect — A Summary
Session 2: The Professional's Role
Session 3: The Multidisciplinary Team Approach
Session 4: The Multidisciplinary Team Approach — continued
from Session 3

Session 1: Child Abuse and Neglect — A Summary

The first session of Module VII will summarize the factors involved in child abuse and neglect. This summary will lay the foundation from later sessions which deal with the multidisciplinary or team approach to abuse and neglect. The session will begin with a brief overview of the module content and the module objectives in order to provide continuity and direction to the sessions that follow.

Content Material: Module Objectives.

Lecture Guidelines: Part 1

I. Summary
   A. Background
      1. Child abuse is not a new or recent occurrence.
      2. Children have been physically and emotionally abused, exploited, sexually molested, and murdered by their caretakers throughout history.
      3. Child rearing practices are relative to time, society, and culture.
      4. Only in the last hundred years has society moved from the idea of children as their parents' property to the concept of children's rights.
      5. In 1974, Congress sighed into law the Child Abuse Prevention and Treatment Act (P.L. 93-847) which mandated that all 50 states adopt legislation requiring persons to report suspected cases of abuse to authorities. It created a National Center for Child Abuse and Neglect.

6. Some researchers now believe that child abuse has reached epidemic proportions.
7. Sexual abuse is happening at an alarming rate.
8. Education and training are focusing public and professional attention on the problem, its prevention and treatment.

Discussion Questions: Part 1

1. How does society's view of children relate to the problem of abuse and neglect?
2. What practices throughout history may have condoned or even encouraged abuse and neglect of children?
3. What are your feelings about these practices?

Lecture Guidelines: Part 2

I. Extent
  A. Factors involved in determining extent.
    1. Defining abuse and neglect is difficult, since perceptions of what constitutes abuse and neglect differ with time and culture.
    2. Currently, all 50 states have enacted statutes requiring mandatory reporting of abuse and neglect.
    3. The definition varies from state to state and from jurisdiction to jurisdiction.
    4. The incidence of child abuse and neglect is unknown.
    5. Estimates vary because of differences in individual perceptions and definitions of abuse, the method data collection, the availability of community resources, and the different methods of research.
    6. The incidence rate should not be based on reported cases alone, since many cases go unrecognized, untreated, and, therefore, unreported.
    7. Although estimates of abuse vary, they reveal that the maltreatment of children is a more widespread problem than it is reported to be.
    8. Estimates suggest that the problem may be of staggering, world-wide proportions.

Discussion Questions: Part 2

1. Do you feel that reporting laws are the answer to case finding?
2. Why is it often said that the incidence of abuse is unknown?
3. What is the correlation between the working definition of abuse/ neglect and the handling of cases?

Lecture Guidelines: Part 3

I. Some factors of abuse and neglect.
   A. Researchers have identified a combination of factors that in the presence of stress contribute to abuse and neglect.
      1. A parent under stress.
      2. A child being seen as different or difficult.
      3. A stressful situation.
   B. Different types and degrees of abuse and neglect exist.
      1. Physical abuse may range from slapping, burning, and beating to murder.
      2. Sexual abuse may range from exposure and fondling to pentration, incest, and rape.
      3. Emotional abuse may be the result of inadequate parenting and severe criticism.
      4. Neglect implies physical, emotional, medical, or educational deprivation.
   C. The effects of maltreatment on children are many and varied.
      1. Prolonged deprivation can have a lasting impact on the child's future development.
      2. The abused child may be the abusive parent of the next generation or the juvenile delinquent or criminal of his generation.
   D. Child abusers come from:
      1. All socioeconomic strata.
      2. Urban, suburban, and rural communities.
      3. A variety of educational levels.
      4. All I.Q. levels.
      5. A variety of racial and religious backgrounds.
   E. Two common myths about abuse are:
      1. Abuse and neglect are problems of the poor.

2. Abusive parents simply misjudge their strength while discipling their children.

F. Poor and nonwhite families tend to be reported more often than upper- and middle-class families for a variety of social and economic reasons.

G. Sexual abuse is becoming a more frequently reported form of abuse.

Discussion Questions: Part 3

1. With what kinds of abuse and neglect are you familiar?
2. What do you think are some of the effects of abuse and neglect on the growth and development of a child?
3. Why are more incidents of abuse reported from lower socioeconomic groups?
4. Is there a typical abuser?
5. To what do you attribute the increased incidence of sexual abuse reporting?

Lecture Guidelines: Part 4

I. Abuse and neglect stages of progression.
   A. A typical child abuse case may involve five stages:
      1. Identification — reporting.
      2. Intake — investigation.
      3. Assessment — disposition.
      4. Treatment — referral.
      5. Termination — follow-up.
   B. Reporting laws and the procedures for managing cases of child maltreatment vary in different states.
   C. A general case flow process exists for all cases of abuse and neglect.
      1. The act of identification by the mandatory reporting laws does not solve the basic problem.
      2. Removal of the child or criminal prosecution of the abuser will not cure the problem.
      3. Identification must be supplemented with investigative tools and intervention.

      4. Intervention and disposition may involve a treatment plan for the abuser, the child, and the family.

D. The comprehensive planning needed for more effective abuse and neglect case handling involves the combined resources of the courts, police, social service organizations, and medical facilities.

      1. Child abuse affects and is affected by society.

      2. It is not only a family problem, it is a social, legal, moral, and medical issue.

      3. Child abuse concerns not only the child and the abuser; it involves professionals, citizens, neighbors, and friends, interested in human services.

E. Some states provide for interagency information sharing procedures.

      1. In many states, the list of persons who may have access to confidential information includes law enforcement officals.

      2. Child Protective Service may provide information for law enforcement officials in cases involving the death of a child, sexual abuse or exploitation, or abuse perpetrated by persons not related to the victim.

      3. Some states have laws that encourage Child Protective Services to request law enforcement assistance, when needed, in conducting an investigation.

Discussion Questions: Part 4

1. What are some of the stages in a child abuse case flow?
2. What role can law enforcement take in any or all of these stages?
3. Under what circumstances would criminal prosecution by advisable?
4. Under what circumstances would criminal prosecution not be advisable?
5. How do you feel about your professional, moral, and ethical responsiblity to help children in cases of abuse and neglect?

Film — *Cry of Pain*, a color film, 15 minutes, 1978. Available from the Pennsylvania Department of Public Welfare, Welfare Press and Publications Office, Harrisburg, Pennsylvania 17120.

Discussion Questions for the film:

1. What are your impressions of the abusive parents?
2. How do you feel about the abusive parents?
3. What are some of the positive approaches to abuse used in the film?
4. Do you see child abuse as a family problem and/or a social problem?

Method of Presentation

The lecture technique will be used along with class discussions in this session. The lecture will stimulate intermittent discussion of the points being reviewed. The lecture guidelines for summarizing and reviewing the background, extent, and causal factors of abuse will serve the trainer as a framework to be augmented according to the needs of the group and as time allows.

The film, *Cry of Pain*, will be shown to reinforce the ideas presented in the lecture and discussion. An introduction to the film will include discussion questions for the learners to consider as they view the film. After the film, the group will discuss their answers to the questions and their reactions to the film content. These questions are to provoke thought during the film and the discussion after the film. The trainer should obtain and preview the film well in advance of its use as a teaching aid in Module VII, Session 1.

Session 2: The Professional's Role

This session reviews the professional's role in child abuse and neglect cases. This material will reinforce the learnings of previous modules and pave the way for the sessions that follow. This material will coordinate the role of many professionals, leading in to the discussion of multidisciplinary teams.

Lecture Guidelines: Part 1

I. In most states, Child Protective Services have the primary responsibility for child abuse and neglect prevention and treatment.

   A. Because child maltreatment is a complex problem, many

agencies are recognizing the advantages of cooperation and coordination with Child Pretective Service Staff. This cooperation and team work:

1. Ensures the protection of the child.
2. Can greatly reduce friction between agencies.
3. Can streamline the investigative process.
4. Enchances the services provided to the family in crisis.

B. A first step in providing this support to Child Protective Services should be the establishment of policies and procedures that give direction and commitment to professional involvement in cases of abuse and neglect.

C. These procedures should assist the learners in identifying and responding to child abuse and neglect.

D. Child abuse units may be formed, consisting of specially trained professionals to work with Child Protective Services in investigating reports of abuse and neglect.

   1. A community wide child abuse unit can be effective in working routinely with:
      a. Schools.
      b. Hospitals.
      c. Mental health facilities and Child Protective Services.
   2. A child abuse unit can be used to:
      a. Gather information.
      b. Provide staff training.
      c. Refer a case to the proper facility.
   3. A child abuse unit would be familiar with:
      a. Community resources for emergency medical treatment.
      b. Emergency placement facilities.
      c. Emergency social services.
   4. A child abuse unit is equipped to respond quickly and effectively at any hour of the day or night because of their special training.

Discussion Questions: Part 1

1. How can the responsibilities of professionals in abuse and neglect investigations be clarified to improve interagency cooperation?

2. Why is it important to train professional personnel in child abuse and neglect investigations?
3. What kind of training do you feel would be helpful to you in your work environment?

Lecture Guidelines: Part 2

I. Police role.
   A. Police involvement in child abuse and neglect cases may require an officer.
      1. To call upon or assist Children and Youth Service personnel during an investigation.
      2. To work with Children and Youth Services in checking on a reported incident.
   B. Because of their differences in approach and perspective, the relationship between Social Service and police personnel are sometimes strained.
      1. In some communities, this strain has been reduced by improved communication and understanding.
      2. To achieve this cooperation, a mutual understanding and, at the very least, a mutual tolerance of social services for law enforcement must be accomplished.
      3. The underlying philosophies and beliefs of these two agencies are different enough to cause a degree of mistrust and misunderstanding.
      4. Two general views exist concerning the approach to the problems of child abuse and/or neglect:
         a. The punitive approach views child abuse as a crime for which parents must be punished.
         b. The therapeutic approach views the problem as a family crisis requiring a treatment plan for the whole family.
      5. The approach of Child Protective Services has over the years gradually moved from the punitive to a theraputic approach.
      6. The current view is that treatment of rehabilitation, rather than punishment and retribution are the best means of child protection.
      7. The law enforcement approach to abuse and neglect

has also changed over the years and is still changing.

8. Law enforcement still believes that pertinent laws must be enforced, but law enforcement has also recognized the need to refer cases of abuse and neglect to those facilities and agencies concerned with rehabilitation and treatment of families in crisis.

Discussion Questions: Part 2

1. What is your perception of the Child Protective Service worker's role in child abuse and neglect cases?
2. How do you think Child Protective Service workers view their role in these cases?
3. How does the role of Child Protective Service workers affect your attitude toward them?
4. In your opinion, what are some commonly held attitudes of Child Protective Services toward law enforcement officers involved in cases of abuse?
5. In your opinion, how do child protective workers view your role in abuse cases?
6. Would a child protective service worker assigned to the police department help improve interagency cooperation?
7. If so, how?
8. Would joint investigative procedures help to improve interagency cooperation?
9. If so, how?

Lecture Guidelines:

I. Summary
   A. When an understanding exists between disciplines.
      1. Several agencies may appoint specially trained personnel to work with and assist Child Protective Services.
      2. The agencies may work together according to appropriate agency requirements.
      3. The agencies may cooperate on disposition decisions.
      4. The agencies may confer on the need for criminal prosecution.

> 5. Interagency cooperation would eliminate a duplication of effort and better serve the child and the family in crisis.

Method of Presentation

The lecture method will be used to present the material. Leader-initiated discussion questions will promote group participation and provide immediate feedback to help the trainer to assess the learning and to determine the need for additional content materials.

The intermittent use of discussion questions and lecture material will reinforce the learner's knowledge about the professional's role in cases of abuse and neglect. These questions are designed to examine and clarify the attitudes and values of the learners in relation to Child Protective Service Personnel.

Session 3: The Multidisciplinary Team

The material in Session 3 and 4 will deal with the multidisciplinary team approach to child abuse and neglect cases. In previous sessions, the importance of cooperation between agencies was stressed. In the following sessions, this idea is extended to include the professional's role on multidisciplinary teams, their response to abuse and neglect, and the need for child advocavy.

All agencies agree about the need to help and protect children. Each profession has its own role, task, and perspective in approaching the problem. A multidisciplinary team approach involves a cooperative effort that results in more effective case management.

Sessions 3 and 4 should have a social work professional as the instructor. Social workers work in conjunction with a variety of facilities and agencies in identification, intervention, and disposition of suspected abuse and/or neglect cases. A social work professional would bring an important dimension to the material. Moreover, this contact between Human Service Agencies could establish a better working relationship between groups.

Lecture Guidelines:

I. The multidisciplinary team approach.

    A. Child abuse and neglect are not solely legal, social, psychological, or medical problems and should not be managed by one discipline alone.

1. They are complex problems that involve intervention by judges, police officers, social workers, lawyers, physicians, and educators.
2. In answer to this complex problem, several jurisdictions have formed multidisciplinary child protection teams to:
   a. Investigate.
   b. Assess.
   c. Treat cases of abuse and neglect.
3. The management capacity and implementation of these teams varies in different counties and states.
4. They most commonly include the skills of legal, social work, mental health, law enforcement, and medical professionals.
5. The teams collective expertise provides a comprehensive and valuable guide for the individual caseworker, investigator, or judge.
6. The implementation of these teams can serve to improve communication and trust between agencies.
7. When understanding and communication exist between the disciplines, cooperation is more easily accomplished.
8. Open communication is essential to early identification of abusive families.
9. The exchange of information, to the extent that it is permitted by law, between medical personnel, Child Protection Agencies, law enforcement departments, and probation officers is important in effective case management.

Discussion Questions:

1. What is the goal in cases of child abuse and/or neglect?
2. In what way are child abuse cases complex and mulifaceted?
3. Why are so many different professionals involved in cases of abuse?

4. What can result from a lack of communication between disciplines?
5. What experiences have you had with formal and informal team efforts in cases of abuse?
6. In your opinion, how might those efforts have been improved?

Discussion Questions:

1. What are some solutions to the problem of abuse that are suggested in the film?
2. What are some of the community resources that are utilized?
3. Have you had any experiences with Parents Anonymous groups?
4. Were they productive?
5. How does the film give you insight into the theraputic approach to child abuse and neglect cases?

A Chain to be Broken is a color film, 28 minutes long, available through the Pennsylvania Department of Public Welfare, Welfare Press and Publication Office, Audio Visual Section, Harrisburg, Pennsylvania.

Method of Presentation

A social work professional, who deals with cases of child abuse and neglect in the community resource system, should conduct or assist the trainer in conducting Sessions 3 and 4 dealing with the multidisciplinary approach to child abuse and neglect.

Content material provided for Sessions 3 and 4 may be used by the trainer or social workers as a framework to be expanded and augmented. The content material provided for Sessions 3 and 4 includes lecture guidelines for the presentation of new material. Discussion questions will reinforce the learning of new material, provide immediate feedback for the instructor, and enable learners to relate the information to their personal experiences.

The film, *A Chain to be Broken*, will emphasize and reinforce the idea that contributions are made by a variety of professionals in helping families in crisis. An introduction to the film should include some points to watch for in the film. The showing of the film should be followed by the discussion questions.

Session 4: The Multidisciplinary Team — continued

This session continues the topic of Session 3, which relates to the multidisciplinary team approach to the problems of child abuse and neglect. Some current operative team approaches will be explored.

The learners involvement in a community wide approach, and advocacy for the protection of children will be considered in Session 4.

Lecture Guidelines:

I. Interagency involvement in a community response to abuse and neglect.

　　A. Child abuse and neglect are community problems which require community solutions.

　　　　1. Cooperative efforts among law enforcement, Child Protective Services in combination with other community agencies can be effective in dealing with these problems.

　　　　2. Because law enforcement officers work so closely with the courts, cooperation should exist between police and the judical system.

　　　　3. Cooperation between community resources can result in efficient, cost-effective case management.

　　　　4. Duplication of services can be avoided.

　　　　5. Many communities are turning to multidisciplinary child abuse and neglect consultation teams, coordinating committees, or task forces as a means of assuring intergrated planning and service delivery.

　　　　　　a. These teams include representatives from Child Protective Services, health, mental health, law enforcement, and education agencies.

　　　　6. All agencies should make an effort to participate on these teams.

　　　　7. These teams may also include representatives from parent self-help groups:

　　　　　　a. Parents Anonymous.

　　　　　　b. Parents United.

8. These teams discuss broad community issues such as:
   a. Available resources.
   b. Sources of funding.
   c. Training.
   d. Public awareness.
9. These teams discuss individual cases:
   a. The best treatment plan.
   b. Dispositional alternatives.
10. These teams consist of members from a wide range of backgrounds, skills and experiences. They meet regularly and can call upon a wide variety of resources, skills and programs to aid families at risk.
11. Consultation teams and community resource committees may serve as a forum for the discussion of social issues. These problems must be addressed by a variety of public and private agencies.
12. Human Service Agencies must be available to participate in these important community programs in order to be a part of the planning and resource allocation.

B. An example of this team community effort on behalf of physically abused, neglected, and sexually abused children is the SCAN Program of Children's Hospital of Pittsburgh. SCAN refers to Suspected Child Abuse or Neglect Cases.
   1. SCAN meetings are held on a regular basis to evaluate suspected cases of abuse and neglect.
   2. SCAN Program recommendations for case management are described in a handbook for hospital personnel.
   3. The hospital has a sexual abuse and rape protocol manual developed in consultation with:
      a. The interagency task force on Rape-Related Services.
      b. Center for Action Against Rape.
      c. The Center for Victims of Violent Crime.
      d. Human Service Agencies.

C. Training is an important part of a community's child abuse and neglect response system.

1. All professionals who work with children or who must report suspected cases should receive training in the recognition, identification, and referral of abused and neglected children.
2. This includes training for all staff, not just professional staff.
3. Nonprofessional staff, volunteer workers, and the public should be aware of the signs and symptoms of abuse and neglect.
4. Neighborhood patrol officers should be aware of children who are consistently unsupervised, uncared for, sleeping outside in bad weather, or stealing food or clothing.

D. Human Service Agencies should take part in public awareness programs through community organizations by providing speakers who can educate the public about abuse and neglect.
   1. Professionals should initiate a move to increase public awareness of the problem and its far-reaching ramifications.
   2. One of the primary functions of a community response system should be the prevention of abuse and neglect.
   3. Professionals vigorously support preventive measures for abuse as it does crime prevention in general.
   4. Professionals can be advocates for prevention of abuse and neglect.
   5. Human Services advocacy can take the form of:
      a. Educational programs.
      b. Improved services for families.
      c. Improved planning and service delivery between all community resource agencies.
      d. Improved communication between agencies.

Discussion Profile:

A community resource task force is being formed to coordinate the efforts of a variety of agencies in working with abused and neglected children. A planning meeting is being held, and these professionals have been invited:

   a. An attorney.
   b. A police officer.
   c. A physician (pediatrician).
   d. A social worker from Children and Youth Services.
   e. A representative from Parent's Anonymous and Parents United.
   f. A psychologist.

Discussion Questions to Consider:

1. As a Health Care Agency representative, what kind of preparations would you make before the meeting?
2. What kind of information would you want to have before attending the meeting?
3. What contributions could you make to a meeting of this kind?
4. What kind of contribution would you be able to make to the task force?
5. Would your attitude be positive about the meeting?
6. Would your attitude be negative about the meeting?
7. In what way would the training you have received during this series of modules help you to contribute to the task force?

Method of Presentation

The material in this session is a continuation of the topic introduced in the previous session. The recommended presenter is a social work professional. The lecture and discussion methods are used to present new information. A discussion case and accompanying discussion questions are provided as a way to summarize the information presented in the lectures. The last two questions of the discussion case are designed to introduce an open question-and-answer session regarding the group's reaction to the modules' content and presentation. The instructor must carefully note the comments and reactions of the learners so that constructive changes can be tailored to the needs of the learners. Such immediate feedback will improve future presentations.

Resources: *Required for the Instructor as Background for Teaching Module VII*

1. Broderick, J.J., *Police in a Time of Change*. New Jersey: Silver Burdette, 1977.

This text describes the role of the police officer in a changing society. A good source of background material for several of the modules, the text particularly relates to Module VII where a changing approach to the protection of children is stressed.

2. Brooker, C.D., and Sommen, R.M., Developing Community Concern with Children. *International Journal of Child Abuse and Neglect*. Pergamon Press Ltd., 3, 1979.

This article stresses the community service approach to child protection, while building a case for the rights of children and the responsibility of the community for promoting child advocacy.

3. Calhourn, J.A. (ed), *Working Together: A Plan to Enhance Coordination of Child Abuse and Neglect Activities*. U.S. Department of Health and Human Services, Office of Human Development Services, Administration for Children Youth and Families, Children's Bureau, National Center on Child Abuse and Neglect, 1980.

While the primary focus of this plan is on federal activities, this publication emphasizes that child abuse and neglect can only be prevented and treated when communities organize, coordinate, and carry out preventive and child protective programs.

4. Eberling, N.B., and Hill, D.A. (Eds.), *Child Abuse: Intervention and Treatment*. Acton: Publishing Sciences Group Inc., 1975.

This text contains articles by a variety of professionals who suggest ways in which intervention and treatment of abuse can be facilitated by the multidisciplinary approach to this complex issue.

5. A film, 28 minutes long, *A Chain to Be Broken*, color, 1978, is distributed by the Pennsylvania Department of Public Welfare, Welfare Press and Publications Office, Health and Welfare Building, Harrisburg, Pennsylvania 17120.

CONCLUSION

THE protection of children from abuse and neglect is of concern to the whole of society. The recent recognition and attention given to this topic documents the publics' interest in what has been labeled a national tragedy.

Among the most important issues challenging professionals who deal with children is one of understanding and awareness of the phenomenon of sexual and physical abuse. Attitudes and a basic knowledge can make a considerable difference in the way one approaches the problem of abuse and neglect of children. Informed professionals and a communitie's attitudes provide a climate that make the difference between good, bad, and mediocre service to the child and his family.

Many professionals are unclear on how to deal with cases of abuse and in the past have preferred to steer clear of involvement. Fortunately, there is a lessening of reluctance on the part of educators and prefessionals in the human services field to recognize and report physical and sexual abuse.

In the past few years, there has been a startling, though long overdue, increase in the amount of interest in Child Protective Services. As this awareness of the problem grows, the desire for education, knowledge and understanding increases. With prevention as the goal, then education should be an important mean to this end.

BIBLIOGRAPHY

Bard, M.: The role of law enforcement in the helping system. *Community Mental Health Journal*, 1971, 7,2: p. 151.

Bard, M.: *The Function of Police in Crisis Intervention and Conflict Management*. U.S. Department of Justice, L.E.A.A. Washington, D.C., Criminal Justice Associates, Inc. 1975, p. 7.

Ibid, p. 8-9.

Bevis, E.O.: *Curriculum Building in Nursing: A Process*. St. Louis, C.V. Mosby Co., 1973, pp. 171-173.

Ibid, p. 181.

Bloom, B.S.: (Ed.), *Taxonomy of Educational Objectives*. Handbook I Cognitive Domain. New York, David McKay, 1974, p. 25.

Briggs, L.J.: *Handbook of Procedures for the Design of Instruction*. Pittsburgh, American Institute for Research, 1970, p. vii.

Broadhurst, D.D.: Project protection, a school program to detect and prevent child abuse and neglect. *Children Today*. May-June, 1975, pp. 22-25.

Broderick, J.J.: *Police in a Time of Change*. New Jersey, Silver Burdette, 1977, p. 81.

Ibid, PP. 181-187.

Ibid, p. 179.

Brooker, C.D. and Sommen, R.M.: Developing community concern with children. *International Journal of Child Abuse and Neglect*. Pergamon Press Ltd., 1979, *3*, pp. 715-723.

Chase, N.F.: *A Child is Being Beaten*. New York, Holt, Rinehart and Winston, 1975, pp. 55-61.

Christy, D.W.: Public concern for abused children. *A National Symposium on Child Abuse*. Denver, The American Humane Association, 1972, pp. 34-35.

Ibid, p. 38.

Cohen, B. and Chaiken, J.: *Police Background, Characteristics and Performances*. Washington, D.C., Department of Justice, 1972, p. 187.

Cohen, S.J. and Sussman, A.: The incidence of child abuse in the United States, *Child Welfare. 54* (6) 432-440, June, 1975.

Community Mental Health Journal, Volume 14 (3) Human Sciences Press, 1978, pp. 101-104.

Cumming, E., Cumming, I. and Edell, L.: Policeman as philosopher, guide and friend. *Social Problems*, 12, 1965, pp. 276-286.

DeFrancis, V.: Protecting the abused child-a cordinated approach. A National Symposium on Child Abuse. Denver, American Humane Association, 1972, pp. 6-9.

Ibid, pp. 12-13.

Dillman, D.A.: *Mail and Telephone Surveys the Total Design Method.* New York, John Wiley and Sons, 1978, p. 86.

Drotar, D., Malone, C. and Negray, J.: Psychosocial intervention with families of children who fail to thrive. *International Journal of Child Abuse and Neglect*, Volume 6 (2) Great Britain, Pergamon Press Ltd., 1979, pp. 927-935.

Eberling, N.B. and Hill, D.A. (Eds.), *Child Abuse: Intervention and Treatment.* Acton, Publishing Sciences Group Inc., 1975, pp. 23-27.

Elmer, E. *Children in Jeopardy.* Pittsburgh, University of Pittsburgh, Press, 1967, pp. 70-72.

Elmer, E., Evolution of children's rights and implications for present policy. *International Journal of Child Abuse and Neglect.* Volume 4 (2) Great Britain, Pergamon Press Ltd., 1979, pp. 917-925.

Elmer, E.: *Fragile Families, Troubled Children.* Pittsburgh, University of Pittsburgh, Press, 1977, pp. 68-84.

Foley, T.S.: *A Review of the Literature on Rape in The Development and Evaluation of the Instructors Manual of Nursing Care of Victims of Rape.* University of Pittsburgh Press, Doctoral Dissertation, 1979.

Fontana, V.J.: *The Maltreated Child.* Springfield, Charles C Thomas, 1971, pp. 17-19.

Ibid, pp. 233-234.

Ibid, pp. 235-236.

Fontana, V.J.: *Somewhere a Child is Crying: Maltreatment Causes and Prevention.* New York, MacMillan Publishing Co., 1973.

Fowler, J. and Stockford, D.: A study of abused children and their parents. *International Journal of Child Abuse and Neglect.* Great Britain, Press Ltd., Volume 3, 1979, pp. 851-856.

Gagne', R.M.: *The Conditions of Learning.* New York, Holt, Rinehart and Winston, 1977, p. 284.

Ibid, p. 286.

Gelles, R.J.: *The Social Construction of Child Abuse.* New York, Harper and Row Publishers, 1975, pp. 363-371.

Ibid, pp. 23-98.

Ibid, pp. 428-429.

Gil, D.G.: *Violence Against Children.* Cambridge, Harvard University Press, 1970, p. 186.

Goldsmith, J. and Goldsmith, S.S. (Eds.), *The Police Community.* Palasades, Palasades Publishers, 1974, pp. 154-156.

Gordon, R.R.: An attempt to reduce incidence of N.A.I. *International Journal of Child Abuse and Neglect*. Great Britian, Pergamon Press Ltd., Volume 3, 1979, pp. 795-801.

Gray, J.D., Christy, A., Dean, J.G., and Kempe, C.H.: Prediction and prevention of child abuse. Journal of Child Abuse and Neglect, Pergamon Press Ltd., 1977, *1*: pp. 45-58.

Green, A.: Sociology: *An Analysis of Life in Modern Society*. New York, McGraw Hill, 1960, p. 539.

Grunlund, N.E.: *Individualizing Classroom Instruction*. New York, MacMillian Publishing Co., 1974, pp. 27-29.

Guthrie, in Eberling, N.B. and Hill, D.A. (Eds.), *Child Abuse: Intervention and Treatment*. Acton, Publishing Sciences Group, Inc., 1975, p. 162.

Helfer, R.E. and Kempe, C.H. (Eds.), *The Battered Child*. Chicago, The University of Chicago Press, 1968, pp. 45-48.

Ibid, pp. 3-17.

Ibid, p. 188.

Ibid, pp. 189-190.

Ibid, pp. 206-209.

Holmes, M.B., project director. *Child Abuse and Neglect Programs: Practice and Theory*. Rockville, Department of Health, Education and Welfare Publication Number (ADM) 78-344, 1978, p. 3.

Hurlock, E.B. Ph.D.: Child Development, 4th ed. New York, McGraw Hill Co., 1956, pp. 20-24.

Ibid, pp. 67-71.

Iannone, N.F.: *Supervision of Police Personnel*, 3rd ed. New Jersey, Prentice Hall, Inc., 1980, p. 333.

Interdisciplinary Glossary on Child Abuse and Neglect. Dept. of Human Services, Office of Human Resources, Administration for Children, Youth and Families. National Center for Child Abuse and Neglect. Sept. 1978, revised 1980.

James, H.: *The Little Victims*. New York, David McKay Co., Inc., 1975, p. 89.

Johnson, D.: *Interpersonal Effectiveness and Self-Actualization in Reaching Out*. Englewood Cliffs, Prentice Hall, Inc., 1972, pp. 15-18.

Justice, B. and Justice, R.: *The Abusing Family*. New York, Human Sciences Press, 1976, pp. 260-263.

Kempe, C.H.: Approaches to preventing child abuse. *American Journal of Disease of Children*. (*130* Sept. 1976).

Kempe, C.H. et al.: The battered child syndrome. *Journal of the American Medical Association*. July 7, 1962, p. 17.

Kempe, C.H. and Helfer, R.E. (Eds.): *Helping the Battered Child and His Family*. Philadelphia, J.B. Lippincott Co., 1972, pp. 10-14.

Ibid, pp. 242-246.

Ibid, p. 30.

Ibid, p. 186.

Kempe, C.H.: The pediatrician's role in child advocacy and preventive pediatrics. *American Journal of Diseases of Children*, (*132* March, 1978), pp. 256.

Ibid, p. 257.

Ibid, p. 258.

Ibid, p. 260.

Kempe, J.E.: Instructional design: *A Plan for Unit and Course Development*. Belmont, California, Fearon Publishers, 1971, pp. 75-85.

Kempe, R.S. and Kempe, C.H., *Child Abuse*. Cambridge, Harvard University Press, 1978, pp. 5-7.

Ibid, pp. 114-119.

Kerlinger, F.N.: *Foundations of Behavioral Research*, 2nd ed. Chicago, West Publishers, 1979, pp. 480.

Ibid, p. 483.

Ibid, p. 548.

Kerper, N.B.: *Introduction to the Criminal Justice System*, 2nd ed. St. Paul: West Publishing Co., 1979, pp. 412-414.

Ibid, p. 413.

Ketterman, T. and Kravitz, M.: *Police Crisis Intervention*. Washington, D.C.: Institute of Law Enforcement and Criminal Justice, U.S. Department of Justice, 1978, V.

Light, R.L.: Abused and neglected children in America: A study of alternative policies, *Harvard Educational Review*, November, 1973.

Mager, R.F.: *Preparing Instructional Objectives*. Belmont, California, Fearon Publishers, 1962, p. 10.

Martin, M.P. and Klaus, S.L.: *1978 Annual Review of Child Abuse and Neglect Research*. Washington, D.C., U.S. Department of Health, Education and Welfare, 1978, p. 30.

Ibid, p. 31.

Martinez, A.: Statement made before the sub committee on Human Resources, U.S. Senate (April 7, 1977), pp. 173-174.

Manninger, W.W.: *In National Symposium on Child Abuse*: Present and Future. National Committee for prevention of Child Abuse, 1975, pp. 32-34.

McKeachie, W.J.: *Teaching Tips: A Guide Book for the Beginning College Teacher*. Lexington, D.C. Heath and Co., 1978, pp. 14-24.

Ibid, p. 25.

Ibid, pp. 37-38.

Ibid, pp. 114-115.

Minn, P.K.: *Honolulu's Operation Help: Round the Clock Coverage*. Denver, The American Humane Association, 1964, pp. 13-18.

Myren, R.A. and Swanson, L.D.: Police Contacts with Juveniles (2nd revised draft). Washington, D.C., Children's Bureau, Department of Health, Education and Welfare, 1961, pp. 1-4.

National Center on Child Abuse and Neglect, *Child Abuse Case Identification and Reporting*. Washington, D.C., Government Printing Office (1977), p. 6-7.

Ibid, pp. 10-11.

Parke, R.D., in Cook, J.V. and Bowles, R.T. (Eds.), *Child Abuse: Commission and Omission*. Canada, Butterworth and Co., Limited, 1980. pp. 295-312.

Parsons, T.: The normal American family, in Farber, S.M., et al. *Man and Civilization.* New York, McGraw Hill, 1965, p. 44.

Payne, D.: The Assessment of Learning: *Cognitive and Affective.* Lexington, D.C. Heath Co., 1974.

Pennsylvania Law Bulletin (Vol. *10* 25) Harrisburg, Pennsylvania, June 21, 1980, pp. 2457-2550.

Pennsylvania Law 247, *The Child Abuse and Treatment Act, 1974,* Amendments, 1975.

Perry, J. and Perry, E.: *The Social Webile,* 3rd ed. New York, Harper-Row Publishers, 1979, p. 99.

Reposa, R.E.: The mental health team: A training and treatment tool with abusing families. *International Journal of Child Abuse and Neglect,* Great Britain, Pergamon Press Ltd., 1979, *3 (4)*:741-747.

Robinson, J.A.: Interdisciplinary in-service education, *International Journal of Child Abuse and Neglect.* Great Britain, Pergamon Press Ltd., 1979, *2 (4)*:749-755.

Russel, J.D.: *Modular Instruction: A guide to the Design, Selection, and Utilization, and Evaluation of Modular Materials.* Minneapolis, Burgess Publishing Co., 1974.

Schuchter, A.: *Child Abuse Intervention.* Washington, D.C., U.S. Government Printing Office, 1976. p. vii.

Ibid, p. 60.

Simon, S. and Howe, L.W., and N. Kirshenbaum, Values Clarification: *A Handbook of Practical Strategies for Teachers and Students.* New York, Hart Publishing Co., 1978, pp. 241-247.

Smith,C.P. and Berkman, D.S., Frazer W.M.: *A Preliminary National Assessment of Child Abuse and Neglect and The Juvenile Justice System*: The Shadows of Distress. Washington, D.C., 1980, pp. 70-71.

Smith, M.: A practical Guide to Values Clarification. La Jolla, Calif., University Associates, Inc., 1977, pp. 162-175.

Solnit, A.J.: *Child Abuse: The Problem, Family Violence,* Toronto, Butterworths, 1978. pp. 243-251. Eekelaar, J.M., Katz, S.M. (Eds.)

Stevens, B.J.: The teaching-learning process. *Nurse Education.* May/June, 1976, pp. 9-10.

Ibid, pp. 18-20.

Stone, J.L. and Church, J.: *Childhood and Adolescence: A Psychology of the Growing Person.* New York, Random House, 1973, pp. 111-113.

Tyler, R.W.: *Basic Principles of Curriculum and Instruction.* Chicago, University of Chicago Press, 1971, pp. 60-63.

Ibid, pp. 65-68.

Ibid, pp. 80-85.

U.S. Department of Health, Education and Welfare. *1978 Annual Review of Child Abuse and Neglect Research.* Washington, D.C., U.S. Department of Health, Education and Welfare Publication, 1978, pp. 2-3.